Did your landlord r███████████
your security deposit because you left
before the end of your lease?

Have the cleaners ruined your $175 coat
and told you they wouldn't pay because
the reclaiming slip says they're not responsible for losses of more than $10?

Did the appliance store refuse to fix, replace, or refund your money on that
lemon of a dishwasher?

SUE THE B*ST*RDS

"For everybody who has ever been burned by
shoddy goods and services, there exists a fascinating, under-used informal system of justice tailor-
made for the legal problems of the Seventies. It's
the Small Claims Court. And its rulings are as
binding as those of any court.

"The purpose of this book is to arm you with what
you will need to win." —Douglas Matthews

"A comprehensive and indispensable guide for
the consumer." —Erie Times-News

"Chock full of genuinely valuable advice."
—Publishers Weekly

Sue The B*st*rds

Douglas Matthews

A Dell Book

Published by
DELL PUBLISHING CO., INC.
1 Dag Hammarskjold Plaza
New York, New York 10017

Copyright © 1973 by Douglas Matthews
All rights reserved, including the right of reproduction in
whole or in part in any form. For information contact
Arbor House Publishing Co., Inc., New York, New York.
Dell ® TM 681510, Dell Publishing Co., Inc.

Reprinted by arrangement with
Arbor House Publishing Co., Inc.
Printed in the United States of America
First Dell printing—January 1975

To Larissa

CONTENTS

ACKNOWLEDGMENTS

I want to thank all the people who made this book possible, and especially: Roger Fisher of the Harvard Law School for his practical aid, encouragement, and advice; Leah Wortham for her invaluable research assistance; Sue Wymelenberg for her irreplaceable assistance across the spectrum; all the judges, clerks, and court personnel too numerous to mention who were almost unfailingly courteous and helpful beyond the call of duty; to Eleanore Zitani for reliably getting her job done; to "Arnie," "Joe," "Hal," and the others who shared their experiences with me; and to Don Fine and the people of Arbor House for their lost stomach linings, and for managing to be a writer's publishing house and top-notch pros at the same time.

This book is the product of three years of unscientific research, interviews, observations, and pondering about Small Claims Courts, literally across the country. Part of the fun of doing this project was that it was unexplored territory. Despite the vast increase in publicity about the courts, there remain many hidden valleys. I would hope that anyone who runs across or discovers any bum steers will write and share the knowledge.

Douglas Matthews
Boston, Massachusetts
1973

SUE THE B*ST*RDS

PRAEMONITAS, PRAEMUNITAS—

FOREWARNED IS FOREARMED

The purpose of this book is to make you armed and dangerous. Armed with a basic knowledge of your civil rights in the Small Claims Court and how to use them, and dangerous to anyone who would trample upon your civil rights.

There are few things in life quite so infuriating as getting skinned in some minor personal or commercial transaction. It can happen in many ways in our wondrous modern society:

• Your so-called mechanic replaces the battery in your car. But the trouble was really the voltage regulator. A week later, the new battery and the generator burned out. Not his fault, the mechanic says; but he'll give you a good deal and fix it for only $157.13.

• About a week after the second time you notify your landlord that the window lock was broken, someone else discovers it and takes the opportunity to relieve you of your $350 stereo.

• Your ex-roommate still owes you $157.39 for those long distance calls to his heartthrob in Manitoba, and all you get out of him is the mañana treatment.

• Some uninsured bozo crumples the rear end of your car. You collect from your own insurance company, but are still out the $100 deductible.

• The airline loses your suitcase and just plain refuses to pay for the $200 camera you had inside.

• The cleaners ruin your suede jacket and won't replace it, pointing to some gobbledygook small print or a sign on the wall that supposedly limits their liability to $5.00.

• The $229.95 dishwasher self-destructed the first week. The store perhaps even tried to repair it, but the thing is obviously a lemon and you want your money back. Now the store says whatever is wrong with it must be a result of your improper use and refuses to fix the old one, replace it, or refund your money.

• Your landlord for no good reason refuses to return your security deposit. Or, if you're the landlord, your tenant puts enough holes in the walls to use up three security deposits.

• From the looks of your furniture after it arrived, the movers routed it over Niagara Falls in a barrel. Demands for reimbursement fall on deaf ears.

• The bank fails to stop the check you told them to make sure and stop.

• The lawnscaper promises you stately verdant splendor, but you end up with scrubby crabgrass and a cancelled check for $400.

• Or in any one of an infinity of other ways, you find yourself on the short end of the financial stick in some small day-to-day dealings with your fellow *homo-sapiens.*

Sometimes reasoned persuasion can turn the trick for you in these situations, which is always a pleasant surprise. But most of the time heavier artillery is needed. That's when Small Claims Courts come in. When in the course of such human events push comes to shove, the title of this book is the name of the game.

(By the way, it's not only in service and sales transactions that Small Claims Courts come in handy. You have important "civil rights" that you can exercise in Small Claims Courts, as you shall see in Chapter Five.)

In short, then, the legal maxim, pile-driven into the heads of first-year law students, is true: For every wrong, the law provides a remedy. The laws and rules are there, on the books and in the cases, to let you get financial satisfaction from whatever malefactors harm or cheat you.

Generally, however, the rub comes with the dispiriting

hassle involved in putting the courts to use. Ironic as it may be in a society that spends billions of dollars each year to maintain a court system, actually using the courts is for the most part considered out of the question for most people faced with garden variety legal problems.

The plain fact is that in regular American civil courts today, the overhead on justice in terms of time, expense, inconvenience, and maddening frustration is so monumental that only claims running into thousands of dollars are worth the trauma of engaging in the "adversary process." For John and Jane Doe with ordinary consumer problems, recourse to a court of law for the justice it promises is a mockingly theoretical right.

This mess the courts are in has been well publicized, of course, and the result is a pervasive, demoralized, and cynical attitude that justice is unavailable to right everyday wrongs.

The real tragedy of this attitude is that it is dead wrong. It may take this country years to straighten out the court system, but even amidst the present muddle, there exists a fascinating, underused, informal system of justice tailor-made for the legal problems of The Seventies.

Almost everyone has heard of Small Claims Court but few realize what a convenient and potent tool this tribunal can be, particularly in the escalating battle against shoddy goods and services in the American market.

In almost every jurisdiction, there is available to Americans a system of justice that is quick, cheap, and fair. Its informality means that there is no need to get a lawyer into the picture, but its rulings are as legally binding as those of any court. And, as those who have tried it generally agree, it is fun to boot.

A couple of these points bear amplification:

1. There is no need to get a lawyer. As a matter of fact, that is the whole point. Lawyers may have their good points, but they certainly seem to complicate things. In Small Claims Courts, you'll find none of this hereintoforewhereastowit stuff, no arguments over fine

points of procedure. The judge won't stand for it. In fact, some jurisdictions bar lawyers completely. Even if the other side bothers to get a lawyer, you will be at no significant disadvantage. (In fact, in this situation, the judge, who can and does interrupt to ask questions, tends to act as your lawyer. For free, and he's got influence in high places besides.)

2. It is cheap. Generally, it will cost you less than five dollars to get the machinery going. And if you win, the other side usually has to reimburse you.

3. Despite its informality, it is a court of law, presided over by the same judges who handle regular cases; and its rulings are backed up by the same enforcement machinery and legal muscle as those of other courts.

4. It is quick. You can almost always get your case heard in two or three weeks as opposed to months or years of waiting in regular courts.

If the amount you wish to recover is within jurisdictional limits—generally about $500 or so—it is probably worth your while to give it a try. And just knowing that it exists can give you valuable leverage in bargaining for a settlement.

Historically, Small Claims Courts are a legacy of the legal phase of the early twentieth-century Populist movement. It was a high-hopes innovation, aimed at giving the ordinary plaintiff his day in court in small matters otherwise not worth litigating because of the expense and complications of ordinary courtroom procedure. Small Claims Courts are the "People's Courts." Although it has not quite lived up to the great expectations of its founders, and in fact is used mostly by businesses to collect debts, there seems to be little intrinsic reason why Small Claims Courts cannot live up to the ideal its founders had in mind.

Indeed, there seems to be at this writing a mild renaissance of interest in the court among reformers ranging from federal judges to Ralph Nader to Harlem Consumer Groups. Young, hip, and educated persons in particular, who know a good thing when they see it, are discovering the court. As a look at a typical session shows, any citizen, old or young, genius or jackass, can get his grievance heard fairly.

This newfound interest has led to a mild spate of well deserved "How To" publicity spotlighting the Small Claims Court system and procedure.

In many cases, the process works out with all the drawingboard simplicity that the "All-you-have-to-do-is . . ." brand of publicity would indicate. But as you'll find out, all too often, it is not that easy. Particularly when you are up against a savvy opponent, your quest for justice can make the search for the Holy Grail look like a milk run.

For example, there's "Arnie," who provided my first introduction to a number of the dirty tricks and dastardly strategems you'll run across as you read on.

I was introduced to Arnie in New York City. Mini-Arnie's exist everywhere there are opportunities for smart, tough-minded, fast-talking conmen, but probably only in the Big Apple could the type have been honed to Arnie's level. He's a combination of killer instinct, street savvy, and loophole knowhow.

Arnie's basic interest is in screwing people. He has a talent for it, he enjoys it. If it weren't his job, he'd find a way to do it as a hobby. If you get stung by a certain multi-million dollar per year gross retail outfit in New York and take them to Small Claims Court, Arnie is the fellow you will run into.

"Let's face it," explains Arnie. "In about ninety-nine cases out of a hundred, we're flagrantly guilty. We're busy. Honoring warranties costs us time and money. If it's just a little thing, okay; but if it's the sort of major thing that is going to run into more than spare change, then we are likely to start giving the guy the runaround and soften him up. My job is to make him end up thinking he is getting away lucky if we give him a third of what the warranty promises. I wear him down or trap him into taking an unreasonable position that will undermine him in front of the judge."

(Notice Arnie doesn't say "in court," but "in front of

the judge." This stress on the key to winning if you actually do get to court—convincing the human being in black robes that you are acting fairly, reasonably, and honestly and that justice as well as the law is on your side—illustrates how well Arnie understands the process. Learn from Arnie, keep this point in mind. It will come up again.)

Since Arnie is his outfit's big gun, he usually gets into the picture only when attempts at pacifying a disgruntled customer have failed and a Small Claims Court summons has arrived.

One of the marks of a good lawyer is that he never goes to trial if he can avoid it, and like all good lawyers, Arnie understands this. The summons is his signal to begin the Treatment.

The Treatment has two purposes: to keep the case out of court, or, if that fails, to engineer the situation so that the other side will look bad in front of the judge.

The Treatment begins with a Reasonable Offer letter sent registered mail. A typical letter goes as follows:

> Typical Victim
> Sucker Street
> New York City
>
> Dear Sir:
>   Please bring your ————— in as soon as possible so that we may repair it free of charge under the warranty.
>
>   Sincerely,
>
>   Honest Arnie
>   Representative

"The important thing about this letter is that it appears to be an honest and reasonable response to the situation," he points out. "Note the polite and even slightly contrite tone. Of course," he continues, " in the context of the runaround we've already given him, it's not honest and reasonable at all. It's finally an offer to do what we were supposed to do all along, and he has to haul the damn piece of junk in to boot.

"Now the letter really has two main purposes," he says, beginning to warm to the subject. (The horrible thing about Arnie, incidently, besides the fact that he actually exists, is that he's a very likeable guy.) "First of all, the guy might actually bring the machine back and leave it with us. Then we fix it at our leisure so that it will run for a while; if it breaks down again, the warranty might have run out or we might have a better chance at arguing that the machine had been abused. And while we have it in the shop time is ticking away on the warranty and his energy.

"The second purpose is to give us something to undermine his case if I actually have to go down to the courthouse. You see, the worst thing the guy can do is to follow his natural instinct, which is to ignore the letter. Then we've got something to show or threaten to show the judge to establish our bona fide good faith and impeach his. 'We tried our best to straighten out the misunderstanding, Your Honor,' that sort of thing. That piece of paper is mightier than the sword in the courtroom."

So what should the guy do? "There are two answers to that question," Arnie says, really turned on now. "One is what he should do now and the other is what he should have done before he filed the suit. . . ."

There were indeed good answers to that question, as well as effective responses to most of the other ploys in Arnie's arsenal. Talking to Arnie and other participants and observers of Small Claims Courts literally from Boston to California has persuaded me that there are just a finite number of dirty tricks that can be pulled on you in the process.

In fact, in the majority of cases you will get your money with remarkably few dollars or hours invested and also enjoy yourself. Even in the more troublesome cases, taking the right steps is easy; and the financial reward and amusement value of being your own Ralph

Nader should add up to more fun than an evening glued to "The Young Lawyers."

You are, however, significantly more likely to win your case and get your money if you know the practical workings of the system from beginning to end.

The end is not just winning in court, but actually collecting your claim. A "judgment," that is, a court decision in your favor, is not cash in hand. It is more in the nature of a hunting license to go out and collect it, an official determination that you are owed a certain sum of money by a particular party. If, after a reasonable time, the defendant still refuses to pay you, you have the right to engage a sheriff or a marshal to collect it for you, usually at the defendant's expense.

Not only is there a difference between a sheriff and a marshal in technical fact; there is usually a big difference in the service you will get from each in a Small Claims Court case, and choosing the right one is important. (The answer is, as you will see, to choose the sheriff.)

There are enough other examples to fill this little book of pitfalls to avoid and paths to choose in waging your cause. No great feats of intellect or memory are required to put them into practice. It is all a matter of straightforward, common sense. But the difference between knowing and not knowing them can be, and for many people is, the difference between winning and losing. (Over one-third of the judgments in New York City Small Claims Court are not collected.) *Praemonitas, praemunitas*—forewarned is forearmed.

The purpose of this book is to arm you with what you will need to WIN, be it in court or in negotiations backed up by the threat of court. If the job has been done right, reading these pages will give you an understanding of the general workings of Small Claims. The steps you should take to file, prepare, and prove your case; how to present your case and yourself in court; what you will need to do to collect your money after you win; and in so far as possible, how to avoid the various pitfalls you are likely to encounter in the process. Also, along the way, you'll be given a number of hints for dealing with lawyers when settling out of court and strategies on how to drive the best bargain in so doing.

In addition, there is a section designed to give you a feel for some of the legal rights you have and that you should be aware of. Finally, you will learn the constructive uses of spite and be treated to the inspirational examples of a man who took on Ma Bell in SCC and succeeded where all others have failed.

The whole subject is simple enough to be mastered without too much tedium and just complex enough to make it interesting. And win, lose, or draw, following the informal but venerable legal maxim of suing the b*st*rds, is certainly better for psyche, soul, and society than letting yourself get steamrollered without a fight. Suing is better than stewing.

CHAPTER I

BEFORE YOU USE THE SMALL CLAIMS COURT

You should use Small Claims Court when you have suffered some sort of legally recognized harm or injury and:

1. The harm or injury is capable of being measured in money. (See "How Much Should I Sue For?" page 40.)

2. There is some specific person or persons, company or companies, who is responsible for the harm or injury. (See "Whom To Sue," page 33.)

3. You have exhausted alternative means of getting satisfaction. (See below.)

Point three is quite important. Suing somebody, even in Small Claims Court, is rolling in the heavy artillery. It takes time and energy that there is no use expending if the object can be achieved more easily, say, by complaining effectively.

Just as in using Small Claims Court or in almost any other endeavor, there are certain tricks and rules of thumb that increase the chances of getting results in complaining. Even if you don't achieve your goal at this stage, complaining in the right way can help you lay the groundwork that will ultimately help you win your case. So before going any further, it's worth outlining a few techniques that maximize complaint effectiveness, even though most of it will seem to be common sense.

To simplify matters, most of the examples that follow assume that you are complaining to a retail store about a product; but the basic technique is applicable to just about any situation.

The first step is to let your fingers do the walking and try the telephone, which involves the exercise of good telephonesmanship.

When you make a telephone call on a complaint, there is a certain logical procedure that makes for effective communication and convinces the person on the other end of the line that he or she isn't talking to an easily put-off dummy:

1. Identify yourself fully. "This is Chris Jones from over in Consumerville."

2. State your general purpose in calling. "I'm calling about
   - that dishwasher you sold me
   - the repairs you made on the car, house, etc.
   - your dog."

3. Ask to speak to the relevant person. Sales manager, service manager, dog owner, etc. CHOOSING THE RIGHT PERSON TO SPEAK TO IS A VERY IMPORTANT STEP. It can mean the difference between getting satisfaction on the first time around or having to go through a lengthy process. The general rule is that you want to speak to someone with the power to make the decision you want to have made. In a consumer context, usually this is someone in a supervisory capacity rather than the person who sold you the item or performed the service. The supervisor is the man who can get action for you. Incidently, on service or appliances complaints, it's good to call even though you know you will have to bring in the item. You'll get quicker service when you arrive.

4. State the specific nature of the problem.
   - "Dirty water keeps leaking from the left rear corner of the machine, and there's this funny smell of rubber burning."
   - "It rained last night and the roof leaks."
   - "The front end still wobbles."
   - "Your dog just bit me and ripped my $200 suit, not to mention my priceless rear end."

5. Make your demand. Demand? Yes, demand. It will of course be phrased diplomatically, but nevertheless it should convey to the person on the other end of the line the sense that you expect that he or she will immediately drop all other business and take care of

your complaint. Also note that when demanding a specific action, it's a good thing to add in a time limit. Thus:

- "Can you please send a repairman over today to look at it?"
- "Can you get over here and do something about it before the next storm?"
- "I'm going to have to get a new suit right away and I think you should pay for it and the tetanus shots, don't you?"

Note that all of the above demands were stated in a way that: (1) demanded a response from the other side, and (2) conveyed an expectation on your part that you are going to be at the very least disappointed if the demand isn't met.

6. Wait for the answer:

The properly timed pause is one of the greatest weapons of effective telephonesmanship. The human psyche abhors a telephone vacuum. Silence is a contradiction of the very purpose of a telephone call. The absurdity of sitting there, holding the phone, trapped, produces an almost irresistable compulsion to fill the breach. So just shut up and wait. An answer will invariably follow.

Often the answer will be a counter-proposal. That is, the person on the other end won't agree to do exactly what you want, but will make a vague promise of the "We'll-get-to-it-as-soon-as-we-can" ilk.

7. Don't accept such a generality. Press for a commitment by restating your demand so as to require a yes or no answer. A good way to do this is to blithely assume they have agreed to your original demand and pretend to be confirming it.

"So you'll send somebody over today, then."

8. If the answer is no, keep pressing.

"You mean, I'll have to wait until tomorrow?"

The strategy is to make the other side keep refusing specific demands. When the other side finds itself having to say "no" three or four times in a row, the vaguely normal human begins to feel an urge to be able to say "yes" on *something*. All those "no's" are building up sort of a psychological debt that can only be repaid by a "yes" of some sort.

So you continue:

- "Well, how about Wednesday? (No.) You mean I'll have to go through the entire weekend? Gee, you people sure must have a lot of complaints."

9. Get a specific promise with a specific time attached, if at all possible.

"So, you can get someone over here next Tuesday then?"

If the person on the other end says that he or she can't make that commitment, then ask to speak to someone who can.

"Look, I have to know so I can be here. There must be someone who knows."

10. Whatever happens, get a promise as specific as possible. Maybe there actually is no one who can promise the repairman will show up at two o'clock on Thursday. But there must be some time within which they can promise or predict. If all else fails, ask how long it normally takes. (This is an important step because you will want a specific promise to refer to if you have to write them a letter, which will be the next move if things aren't settled to your satisfaction.)

11. Ask who it is you are talking to and write it down. It will give you something else to refer to in any letter you send.

The above implementation of the art of telephonesmanship may or may not get results. If it doesn't you can at least be sure that you have maximized your chances—and made an impression on the other end.

At any rate, if for some reason, things don't work out—the person doesn't come or the repairs are sloppy, or the lemon is just plain unrepairable—it's time to escalate to Phase Two, which is letter writing.

The pen may or may not be mightier than the sword, but it certainly is true that paper is the most important weapon in the consumer arsenal. The first rule is to save all paper. It doesn't take an elaborate filing system. Just shove everything in a big envelope or in a drawer, so you can get your hands on it again. Applying this principle to the letter phase means keep a copy of *EVERYTHING* you send out. These copies will come in handy. If you have access to a xerox machine, fine. If not, use that other marvelous invention, carbon paper. How many copies? Three is not too many.

The copies of the letters you send will be used in demanding further action and ultimately in court, if it comes to that. If you can show the judge that you have made an effort to get satisfaction in a reasonable way and that they broke their promise to deliver it, then you have gone a long way toward getting his sympathy. That is considerably more than half the battle. A good letter lays the groundwork.

The principles of effective mailsmanship parallel quite closely those of good telephonesmanship, since the goals of effective communication and prodding to action are the same. The letter should contain the basic facts:

- When and, if necessary, where you purchased the item or received the service and from whom. If you don't know the name of the salesman, which you probably won't, describe him: "heavyset man with sunglasses and a shiny green suit."
- As specifically as possible, the representations that were made to you, if any, about the quality of the service or the product when they sold it to you. Here you are laying both the moral and legal groundwork for your claim.

Basically, what you are saying is that you were promised such and such specific result or a product that performed up to such and such a standard, or whatever. These representations, if you can prove them, are often legally binding despite disclaimers on guarantees. If the other side doesn't deny them in any answer they may send, there is an inference to be drawn that this silence is an admission, since a chance to deny your allegations was passed up. At the very least, the other side later has to come up with an answer to the question of why they waited until now to deny. And when it's your word against theirs this piece of paper lends extra weight to yours.

This principle of stating any representations made to you is especially important when dealing with a product that technically functions correctly, but is not well-enough designed to do its job. If the salesman said, "Yessirie, this here little brute will get all those dishes sparkling like the Hope Diamond" and the dishwasher sloshes and purrs through its cycle all right but leaves the dishes all crudded up, then you are not asking for repairs but for your money back. And if you bought the machine relying on that inducement, there's no reason why you shouldn't get it back.

- A summary of the story thus far. Your purchase, its date, what went wrong, your telephone call, what was promised over the phone, what happened, why you are not satisfied. Again, be specific but terse. Just the facts, but all the facts are needed. These generally fall into the old "Who, What, When, Where, How and sometimes Why and How often" rule.

- Your demand. This may be a restatement of the old demand, or a new one. "Since your servicemen do not seem to be able to repair it, please make arrangements to replace it or pick it up and refund my money."

What your demand should be depends on a lot of things. From the response of the other side thus far, you should pretty much know how honest and sincere the people you are dealing with are. That and the other circumstances surrounding this whole transaction should let you figure out what the best thing to do is. You can try to have the whole deal called off, the product returned, and your money refunded. Or, if you think it's just your particular one that's a lemon, you might want to have them deliver a new one.

However, in this business of making demands, don't get carried away. Put yourself in the other side's shoes. Ask for something that the other side can say yes to, not something outrageous and that may be used later to make you look unreasonable.

Anyway, no matter what you demand, note that your letter doesn't have to be in lawyer's or businessman's English. Just plain language will do the job and present no danger of making you sound silly if you misuse lawyer's style.

So, a good letter might read like this:

Dear Decision Maker:

On (date), I purchased a (thing) on sale for (price). The set in the store worked fine and the salesman, a dark-haired man whose name I do not have but whom I would recognize, assured me that the set would work right in my house and said that it was "100 percent guaranteed" for six months.

Unfortunately, the set has not worked at all satisfactorily since you delivered it. Everybody's skin is green, the sound is very scratchy, and whenever anyone in the room sneezes, the picture starts flopping. The repairman you sent out (date) in response to my call fooled around with it, and it was a little better for a couple of days. But now it's back to its old tricks. The same thing happened when he came the second time.

Since the set is useless to me in this condition, I think the best thing to do is for you to refund my money and come and pick it up.

Please let me know as soon as you can when we can get this done.

Sincerely,

For extra impression, you can go to the post office and send the letter certified mail, return receipt requested. This will make a psychological impression and give you a signed receipt, forestalling any claim that your letter wasn't received.

Note that the letter is addressed to the "decision maker," that is, that person with the authority and power to make the decision you want to have made. By this stage in your dealings, you should know who that is.

After this, it's up to the other side. If your demand is met, then you've won and it's endgame. Most of the time this is the way it will be. You've made it a lot simpler for the other side to give you what you want within reason than to continue.

But if the other side refuses or ignores your plea, then you can decide to give letter writing one more try or to initiate suit. The decision depends on whether you think the second time around will be effective. By this time, you can tell the sort of person you have been dealing with. It's possible that just a little additional shove will get what you want. Or that no amount of further persuasion will budge them an inch. In that case, push has come to shove.

If you are dealing with a complaint involving a brand name product, it is probably worth one more letter. This one will do three things:

1. State your position and demand once more.
2. Explain that you feel you have no choice but to seek whatever legal recourse may be available to you.
3. Be sent to manufacturer also.

The third step, appealing to a higher authority, puts additional pressure on. In the first place, chances are that the manufacturer will actually be concerned and will contact the store for an explanation. In the second, even before any such action is taken, the local store manager or whomever you've been dealing with may choose to head off any more hassles. Finally, you have one more piece of paper to show that you have been reasonable.

Such a letter might go as follows:

Dear Decision Maker:

As you know, ten days ago I sent you a letter asking to return the television set which has given us so many problems. So far, I haven't received an answer. (Or: I am afraid I can't agree with your letter suggesting that the problems are not covered by warranty or are caused by my misuse of the set.)

I really still feel that the only fair way to resolve this matter is for you to take the set back and refund my money. If you still don't feel this way, then I guess we'll have to settle the matter in court. Please contact me immediately.

Sincerely,

cc: President
     Brand Name TV
         (address)

     previous correspondence
     enclosed.

The decision maker should receive copies of the letter with carbon copies of your first letter enclosed. The third carbon you save for the judge.

One question that arises using this technique is how to find the address of the manufacturer. Most of the time, it's printed somewhere on the product; but if it isn't, you can always drop into the local library and ask at the reference desk for what you want. Almost always, the library will have one or more business directories. Or, if you have a stockbroker, he or she will have handy access to that information. One advantage of going to a business directory is that you can usually get a specific name, which is always better. Otherwise, just go to the top and address it to "President."

There are sources other than the manufacturer you can appeal to, such as the Better Business Bureau, which we will hear of later, or Chamber of Commerce, and these can be used if you are dealing with a local store. But the pressure, if any, engendered by this sort of appeal or even appeal to government bodies such as consumer affairs offices isn't as strong as appealing to someone higher up in the company, if you are dealing with a chain, or directly to the manufacturer.

At any rate, by this time, or perhaps without even going through all these steps, if satisfaction has not been rendered, it's apparent that the time has come to escalate to the most effective means of complaining available to any consumer: Small Claims Court.

CHAPTER II

STEP-BY-STEP: DECISIONS AND TACTICS

FINDING THE COURT

This may not be as trivial a matter as it sounds. Small Claims Courts are rarely listed in the phone book as such, and it is hard to know exactly under what heading to look, even if they are, since a SCC can come under the jurisdiction of any one of a number of governmental levels.

In any event, the way to proceed is first turn to the Appendix in the back of this book. Sometimes even the phone number of your court will be there. If it's not, take your local phone book and start with the listings under "City of." If you hit something called SCC, fine; if not, try the least exalted listing there—something like "Municipal District Court," "Civil Court," or "Civil Session," and call that and ask. If it isn't there, they will know. Or if there was no promising listing under that heading, do the same under county listings. If you don't know what county you live in, call the Post Office and find out.

If for some reason you just become hopelessly confused, pick a lawyer out of the phone book and call. The person who answers the phone will probably know.

WHOM TO SUE

Since, in the absence of complete frivolity, there are virtually no operative sanctions against the shot-gun approach, the general traditional legal strategy is to sue first and ask questions later, "bringing in" to the suit anyone remotely connected with the transaction. This philosophy normally makes strategic sense since two can be sued as cheaply as one, there is often genuine uncertainty as to who is liable for what, and the general principle that people will do anything to save their individual hides, including turning against former associates (the Watergate syndrome).

As a practical matter, however, you'll at least want to consider whether or not your target has anything more than holes in his pocket. You can sue someone on welfare easy as pie, but try to collect and you will discover the meaning of the phrase "judgment-proof."

On the other hand, a judgment is collectable for a long time, usually ten to twenty years. This means you can haul somebody into court once a year for the next ten to twenty years to examine his assets and see if he can afford to pay the judgment, plus all the interest accrued. So, if there's a chance that your target's fortunes will change, it may be worth suing now to get your judgment, even if you know you can't collect. You have to have a bit of the avenging spirit celebrated by Edgar Allan Poe in *The Cask of Amontillado* to keep at it, but the third or fourth year someone is hauled into court for an examination of assets, they tend to offer some sort of settlement.

Generally speaking, if you are suing for a transaction with a business, you want to sue the business rather than the employee, if he was acting in his capacity as employee. If you are in an automobile accident, sue both the driver and the owner so as to bring in the insurance company. If you are in any doubt, by all means sue. And always go after the "deep pocket," the party with the money.

In a way, any advice on the pure strategy of choosing whom to sue is rather artificial. Your real question usually is whom *can* you sue; and that depends on whether you can "serve" your target with a summons. As you will see in the next section, there are many instances where the arm of the law is not very long at all.

SUMMONS SERVING—VENUE AND
PROPER NAMES

A "summons" is the official piece of paper the court sends to someone ordering him to appear at the court on a certain day under pain of penalty. A summons to a defendant is usually accompanied by a "complaint," which informs him of who is suing him and the grounds of the suit against him. In Small Claims practice, the two forms are usually combined onto one piece of paper.

Summons serving is a little like a game of tag. If the summons "tags" you, you are caught and have to go to court on the day it says. But even if the other party knows you are available in the jurisdiction, and you know the other party is trying to serve you, and the other party knows you know they are trying, no one can make you go to court unless it can be proved that the summons has been properly served.

There are two main ways of summons serving in SCC; service by mail and personal service.

Mail service is accomplished by sending the summons by certified mail. The recipient's signature on the letter constitutes proof of service.

In personal service, a sheriff, marshal, constable, or other designated person chases down the victim and hands him the summons, just like in the movies. The process server then signs an affidavit swearing that he has "served" the party designated. (People being what they are, summons servers have been known to fill out the affidavit without serving the summons. This practice, which still occurs, is called "sewer service," after the presumed final resting place of the summons.)

You must not only serve the defendant properly, however, you must also sue him in the right court. This aspect of jurisdiction is called "VENUE." Different states have different provisions. Sometimes a defendant can only be sued in the court within whose district he lives. Sometimes you can sue in the court within whose district he lives or works, or the court within whose district you live. Sometimes you can sue him wherever you can serve him. It all depends and you should check your state appendix and double check with the clerk before wasting a trip to the wrong courthouse.

You must also know a couple of details about your target. First, is it the full and correct name and address? In the case of an individual middle initials aren't necessary, but the first and last name is. Nicknames are no good, either. "Buzzy" Jones probably does not exist in the eyes of the law. Neither does Bob Jones. It's Robert Jones that you want to sue.

In the case of a corporation, this rule also applies. Often, the "DBA" name of a store (the name it is "Doing Business As"), for example, is not its real name. The sign over the door may say Wobbly Furniture Emporium, but the corporation you must sue may be something like Wobbly Merchandising, Inc. If you don't sue them under their real name, including the "Inc.", you will not effect proper service. This means that whenever you sue a business that's incorporated, you will have an extra step, checking out the official name.

One easy way to do this, if the establishment is licensed, is to look at the license, which the law will probably require to be displayed in a prominent place on the wall, and which will be issued in the official name. If this technique is inconvenient or inapplicable, then you're going to have to find the place where the official "DBA" records are stored. This is often the county clerk's office. Or, if you have time, you may be able to just send a stamped self-addressed post card to your state's secretary of state's office. How to find the correct name should be easily obtained from the Small Claims Court Clerk on your first, court-locating, phone call.

The next necessary piece of information is the person's address (home or business, depending on venue rules).

If you want to sue someone whose address you aren't sure of, there are a number of ways of finding it out. There's always the phone book or Information. If that doesn't work, you should try the city directory or police census for your city. This is a big book listing people's addresses. It also does the reverse, listing the names of people according to their addresses. Check a couple if the target is not in the first one. Even an old address might help.

If you have an old address, here's a trick suggested by a professional bill collector. He says you might be able to get it through the Post Office if the target filed a change of address slip. Change of address information is confidential, but try sending a registered letter with a couple of blank sheets in it to a Fictitious Name, care of the target, and with the notation Deliver to Addressee Only. If all goes well, the envelope will not be delivered because of the notation Deliver to Addressee Only; but the envelope, when returned to you, will bear the forwarding address in pencil.

DEALING WITH THE CLERK

Once you have selected your target, identified it properly, pinpointed its location, chosen the proper court, and figured out how much to sue for, it's time for your first trip to the court. You are ready to file your complaint and issue summons.

When you get to the court, you will probably find that the clerk's office consists of a long counter, behind which there are a number of people relentlessly carrying all sorts of papers from point A to point B. On the other hand, clerk of Court personnel are as a group among the most courteous and patient people you will run across in government service.

There seems to be a union rule in clerk's offices that one does not become visible until five minutes of patient standing have elapsed. There being some things you just can't buck, just hang on. Don't get aggressive until a really indecent amount of time goes by. This too shall pass.

When someone finally perceives your presence, tell

him or her you want to file a Small Claims Court case. The clerk will either give you a form to fill out or fill one out with you. He'll ask for: (1) the complete name and address of the defendant; (2) your name and address; (3) the reason you are suing, which he will probably summarize into a short descriptive phrase such as "breach of contract," "personal injury," "negligence," "money owed," or some other short phrase. This is the vestigial remains of the "complaint," and is what the defendant will receive as the reason for being called to court on his summons; (4) the amount for which you are suing; and (5) money (in cash only) for the summons and any other fees. The appendix of this book will give you an idea of how much, but it will normally be less than five dollars.

What you will get from the clerk is: (1) a docket number, which you should not lose, since you will need it anytime you discuss your case with the clerk; and (2) the date for the trial.

You might wish to file your claim on a day when you know the Court is in session, so you can take a peek at the proceedings. But, remember, since you will probably not be getting the same judge, and every judge runs the proceedings differently, there is no guarantee that your trial will be run in the same way as those that day. So it probably isn't that important a thing to do.

One of the jobs of the clerks is to filter out groundless or frivolous suits. This means that if you try anything fancy, you may run into a clerk who will be a little hesitant to take your case. Perhaps a conference with superiors will ensue. The thing to do is to politely but firmly insist that it's something you'd like to take before the judge. If you indicate that you understand this is kind of an unusual suit, but that you think it's the sort of thing that should be brought in Small Claims Court; and that you're willing to take your chances; and do not think you're being irresponsible and wasting the court's time, you can probably convince the clerk to let it through. After all, if you're not a complete wise-off, it's easier for him to let it slide than to make a fuss about it.

If there's any trouble, you should remember that you have a right to file the suit. It's for the judge, not the clerk, to decide whether a suit has legal grounds or not.

About the only thing the clerk can do, if he is convinced that you and/or your case are completely zany, is make you go see a judge to get permission to file suit.

The clerk will explain the Summons procedure of your jurisdiction to you, that is, whether you can serve a summons by certified mail or must hire a process server, or what. One question you should ask him, particularly in a jurisdiction where the summons will be issued by certified mail, is what happens if the summons is not delivered. (Wily targets often refuse to accept a piece of certified mail, knowing full well what it is.)

If the certified-letter route doesn't work, you will have to get a new summons issued and arrange for a personal service, either through a constable or ordinary citizen, such as a friend, depending on the rules of your jurisdiction. If a friend does serve the summons, he will have to swear he did so by signing the affidavit of service in front of a notary public, who will also sign it. Then this form is mailed back to court. Your new summons, of course, will have a new trial date.

One problem with this procedure, however, is that sometimes you are not warned that service has not been accomplished by mail, and you come down to the court on trial day thinking you're finally going to get your judgment, when all you're in for is a wasted trip as the mailed summons was not accepted. Therefore, you should plan some way of finding out before trial whether the summons has been served. In some places you can do this by a telephone call. (Aren't you glad you kept your docket number so the clerk can quickly locate your case?) Other courts, however, will not answer such questions over the phone. Ask the clerk what the story is while you are there; if no telephone queries are accepted, try to leave a self-addressed postcard and ask to have it mailed to you if the summons comes back undelivered.

HOW MUCH SHOULD I SUE FOR?

Usually, the answer to this question will be fairly obvious. Your legal "damages" are equal to the value of what you lost by the other side's illegal act.

But there are a few occasional wrinkles to the general issue of legal "damages" that you should know, although things are considerably simplified by the fact that the upper limit of your suit is fixed by the jurisdictional limit of the court.

You should be able to figure pretty closely what your case is worth if you look over the following rules of thumb.

1. Don't Sue Yourself Short

First of all, almost any "personal" injury, that is, injury to your body, is worth more than the small claims limits because of the money you can collect for "pain and suffering."

I once saw a man sue in a Small Claims Court for a fractured ankle he suffered as a result of a fall on someone's property. For some reason, neither he nor the other side had lawyers nor had consulted one. The man sued for and collected $400. I later asked a lawyer what he should have sued for. The answer was a minimum of $5000. So don't sell the value of your pain and suffering short. If you have a personal injury, always contact a lawyer before taking the matter into your own hands. Otherwise, you may be throwing away money.

This does not mean that you can't cut your claim if you have a lawsuit with damages you are sure of—let's say a debt owed—that's slightly above the limit and you wish to avoid sharing a third with a lawyer and waiting for regular court to get around to hearing the case. If the limit is within 80 percent or more of what you are going to get anyway, you might well be wiser to sue for the limit in SCC.

2. *If property is ruined or destroyed you get "fair market value," not "replacement value."*

Even if you just put $400 worth of repairs into your 1964 Cadillac that you bought for $200, you do not necessarily have a $600 car. You have a car which is on the high end (how was the body?) of the standard "blue book" value for 1964 Cadillacs.

The same principle applies to almost-new items; here you have to keep in mind the concept of depreciation, the fact that an item is worth 10 percent to 30 percent less the instant after you pay for it because it is now secondhand. It costs you several hundred dollars to drive that first mile on your new car, to take an extreme but common example. Even though you bought that dress only three months ago and wore it only once, or even never wore it at all, you shouldn't expect to get exactly what you paid for it, even if you bought it at a 50 percent off sale, and it would now cost you twice as much to get one just like it.

3. *You can collect for out-of-pocket expenses or other financial loss you incurred because of the other side's act—IF:*
   - *you can demonstrate with reasonable certainty that you would not have taken the loss except for the act; and*
   - *it's the kind of loss that is a reasonably forseeable result of the other side's act.*

If, as a result of a mechanic's negligence, your car breaks down in the middle of a freeway, as mine did after someone put the wrong size universal joint in, not only can you get your money back from the mechanic, but the cost of towing and perhaps a couple of days cab-fare. On the other hand, if because of the break-down you miss an appointment and lose a deal, the court would be much less likely to give you damages because you can't really prove that the deal would have been closed that day. Those damages are too "speculative."

Another limitation to the rule that you are entitled to compensation for indirect damages is that you cannot collect for your time that is lost as a result of the breach unless you can show that you lost wages. Thus, the extra time you have to spend going back and complaining, or the time it takes to start and pursue your lawsuit, or in general any other time you wasted because of the defendant's act will generally not be compensated, no matter how annoying.

I once saw a man sue out of fury over a runaround of false information he got from a steamship company. He had been seeing friends off and the steward kept telling him they were in different cabins. After something like two and a half hours of fruitless searching, he was driven into near apoplexy, so he sued. (The friends, incidentally, were on board all the time, wondering where he was.)

The judge listened politely, even sympathetically, but found against him. The man did have the satisfaction of dragging to court a company official and a lawyer armed with all sorts of plans of the ship, and other documents. (It was an evening court session, too.) It seemed to me that this was a case where the catharsis was more important than the cash, so perhaps justice was served. It also seemed that a good lawyer would have settled for a few dollars.

Another form of out-of-pocket expenses that are not recoverable are lawyers' fees.

4. *You have to pay for what you get and keep even if you would prefer to leave things the way they were.*
   This principle often comes into play when you have home repair jobs that aren't quite up to snuff and *you* get sued by the workman. Courts are pretty sympathetic to workmen. They come into court with bills for supplies and claims for days spent. The usual result is the defendant's having to lay out some compromise amount of money on the theory he received that much "benefit" from the bargain.

   You will get some hints on how to deal with workmen later, but just let's point out that your best defense is to call another workman in to get an estimate on how much it would cost to finish the job to your specifications. Then subtract that amount from what you are being sued for and tell the judge that is what you think you should pay.

The general point to remember, however, is that you are going to have to pay for what you get. If you order one pair of shoes, and two arrive, you are probably even under a duty to notify the sender of the mistake and mail the extra shoes back, if he sends you postage. And if you give them to your mother, you have bought them and must pay for them.

5. You have a duty to keep your damages to a minimum.

Just because you have been legally sinned against, it doesn't mean that you have been given a blank check. If someone fixes your roof and it still leaks, you have a duty to move the expensive sofa out of the way as soon as you discover the leak and to put a bucket down. Or if you are a workman and are half-through a job and the person says stop, you should stop. (On the other hand, if there is no other work, you can sue for the full *profit* you would have made on the deal. This is the real measure of what you lost.)

You can think of this duty to "mitigate" damages as part of your general duty to act reasonably.

6. Forget about punitive damages.

Occasionally, very occasionally, the law recognizes that there has been an action so bad that the defendant should literally be punished. Generally this involves some sort of gross willful misconduct. The rationalization is that this punishment will serve as a deterrent to others and that this behavior was especially heinous in view of the defendant's position in the community or whatever.

No matter how exasperating the other side has been, forget about punitive damages in Small Claims Court. I have never seen or heard of them being awarded and some statutes specifically prohibit them. It's just not that sort of game; if you can persuade a Small Claims Court judge to give you punitive damages, drop what you are doing, go to law school and look forward to a brilliant career at the bar.

These general rules should cover the theoretical aspects of most situations you will encounter. When in doubt, sue for the larger amount. There isn't much, if any, harm in asking.

Also, as a practical matter, considerations other than the actual legal damages you are entitled to may influence your decision of how much to sue for. For example, if you're suing for damage to something with a non-standard price, or one that will not be ascertainable by the other side before trial, and you think the other side has an attorney (which most corporations will have), you might consider the wisdom of adding 30 to 40 percent to the value of your claim.

This might be advisable because you will almost certainly get some sort of settlement offer from the other side's lawyer if you have anything resembling a valid claim in the first place. The lawyer doesn't want to bother going to court any more than you do especially for a small amount of money. However, once he realizes you are willing to settle, he's not going to offer you anything close to the real value of the claim at first. He's going to start low. He will, however, probably be quite happy to finish up knocking 30 percent or 40 percent off, particularly if you go through the motions of putting up something of a struggle. If nothing else, his ego will be caressed and his client impressed by the inference that he is a shrewd negotiator. So, if you add 30 percent to your claim and the lawyer offers you about 50 percent, you are really getting closer to three quarters. And if you are a good negotiator . . .

Of course, if the attorney doesn't call you to settle, or if there is no attorney, and no offer of settlement, you are in a rather peculiar position if and when you get to the court.

It is illegal, immoral, and otherwise damaging to your

case to inflate your damages in a court of law. The thing
to do, if you're caught in that bind, is to just tell the
judge the truth. "Your honor, there's a mistake here in
the amount I'm suing for. It's really only X dollars." If
the judge asks for a further explanation, give him the
full story: "All I really wanted was the fair value of
what I lost. I figured that a good lawyer would call me
for a settlement and that I would be able to save time
by compromising. But I was afraid that he would be
a much better bargainer than I am, so I started off high
so that he would have farther to go to get me down
below what I deserved. That's all I really want, what I
deserve."

If you have a reasonable case, the judge is not going
to hold such a maneuver against you. You were young,
it was spring . . .

SHOULD I SUBPOENA ANYONE OR ANYTHING?

A subpoena is a document that the court will issue on
your request that requires the person that receives it
to either (1) come to the trial himself, or (2) bring
specified documents or other evidence to the trial. (This
second form of subpoena is called subpoena duces
tecum.)

Subpoenas must be served, just like summonses.
Therefore, you will run into all the same problems that
surround summons serving. In addition to paying a fee
for serving the party, you will probably also have to pay
something called a witness fee, usually four dollars or
five dollars a day, plus the witnesses' mileage at a rate
of approximately twelve cents to fifteen cents per mile.
If you subpoena a peace officer, you may have to pay his
salary too, plus his reasonable traveling expenses.

These above expenses, while they may be annoying
if you really need a witness and have no other way to
get him there, do at least prevent the landscape from
being littered with subpoenas, which after all are quite
an inconvenience to the recipient.

You will probably rarely need to subpoena anyone. Judges understand that witnesses are reluctant to come to court, particularly for a Small Claims Action, so are accustomed to doing without witness testimony that would be considered required in a regular trial. In addition, unlike a regular trial, signed statements from witnesses otherwise available are perfectly kosher in Small Claims Court. Just write a letter to the person explaining that you do not wish to subpoena him but need his or her corroboration as to certain facts . . . which facts you should list . . . and ask for a return letter. In all probability, it will suffice. At any rate, if you really feel that you need someone to complete your case, you know that you can get him if you can serve him with a subpoena. Also, a subpoena might be useful in a situation when you have a witness who doesn't mind coming, but needs an excuse to give to a third party such as an employer.

Subpoena duces tecum's come in handy if you've lost a sales slip or some other needed document that the other side should have. Third parties can also be served. If it's the kind of record they should be expected to keep, they will have some explaining to do if they don't show up with it, and the onus of your not having the document is somewhat attenuated. You should understand that document subpoenas cannot be used to go on a "fishing expedition." That is, you must specify to a reasonable extent, what it is that you're looking for. If you ask for all documents arising out of a single transaction, for example a sale, you'd probably be okay. However, let's say you're arguing with a bank over a deposit that they didn't record and you do not have a deposit slip. It's doubtful that the court would make them bring all the records of all their deposits for that day, even if it were a very small bank, or even if it involved only a small branch of that bank.

In short, while subpoenas are useful and necessary incidents of regular trials, they are rarely appropriate for Small Claims Court use.

WHAT KIND OF DELAYING OR ESCAPE TACTICS ARE AVAILABLE TO THE DEFENDANT?

There are a number of theoretical ways the defendant can try to delay at this point. The most common will be to ask for a continuance, something we will deal with in detail in Chapter Four.

In addition in some jurisdictions instead of the right to appeal, a defendant gets the right before trial to transfer the action to a regular court. Usually this only costs a few dollars. Often, the procedure consists of an application for a new trial to a higher court, and then a remanding of the cause for trial in Small Claims Court. This paper shuffling accomplishes only one thing for the defendant. It preserves his right to appeal after the Small Claims Court trial. Then he must go through all the hassles described above. However, this is a very good delaying measure, since it can take months for the first application for transfer to be remanded, and years before the trial comes up after appeal. Luckily, few people consider it worth the trouble, and few jurisdictions offer the option.

One other escape mechanism is for the defendant to file a counterclaim. Suing is a two-way street. If the defendant feels that he has a claim against you, he can have it combined with your claim against him by filing a "counterclaim." Once again, this is a device more common in regular trial than in a Small Claims Action. But it comes up once in a while when plaintiffs sue stores they owe other bills to, but haven't paid pending the suit.

You will be notified if a counterclaim is filed against you. About the only real worry this process might present is that a counterclaim in excess of the SCC money limit will cause the action to be transferred to regular court.

Another delaying tactic available to SCC defendants in many jurisdictions is to request a jury trial, which can often take a year or two to come up. Actually, I have never heard of anyone doing this.

Anyone who wanted to ask for a jury trial would have to go through a great deal of hassle posting bonds, filing affidavits and various other forms. If anyone ever made me and eleven other people come to jury duty and sit there on a Small Claims Case, I would vote against him on general principles and try to impose punitive damages. I would hope that all right-thinking Americans would agree.

SHOULD I CONSULT A LAWYER?

If you have a lawyer already, you should by all means consult him. Let him know what happened, what you are planning to do, your preliminary battle plan, and ask him if he has any advice to offer. He can give you good off-the-top-of-the-head advice, and he is certainly not going to charge a regular client for a four or five minute phone call.

Even if you don't have a lawyer, if you are confused or unsure, or feel you need more advice, you can still go in and consult one. Ask around, or call the local bar association, or maybe your bank, to get a name. If you keep your consultation down to fifteen minutes, which you certainly should be able to do, he cannot really charge you more than twenty dollars or so, if he is an ordinary solo practitioner. (You might even be able to do the whole thing over the telephone for free; and even if you are billed, the value of the advice may be well worth it.)

You should not, however, feel that you have to consult a lawyer. This is do-it-yourself justice; the whole purpose of the system is to dispense with the need for professional legal assistance.

HOW SHOULD I DRESS FOR JUSTICE?

One question that comes to mind is whether how you dress will affect the outcome of your case. Short of sewing the American flag on the rear end of your dungarees or otherwise sartorially comporting yourself like Abbie Hoffman, I do not think dress is that important for men, as long as there is some overture toward respect. That is, if you think it's a good way to dress, I think it will be all right with the judge. I have seen really bizarre outfits that had no effect because the wearer obviously considered himself a fashion plate. (I remember this guy in a red plaid jacket, a yellow shirt, long hair, and clunky men's high heels that Italian designers are trying to force on us.) I was waiting for some reaction on the part of the judge, but it was limited to a bemused initial smirk and the young man, who turned out to have his own painting contract business, won his case for money due for painting something.

Again, the important thing is some *shown respect*. If you go in with your black leather jacket and dungarees, shoulder-length hair and beard, that's fine; just make a little show of buttoning up the jacket, smoothing down your hair as you walk up to the bench, and the old geezer may be touched enough to lay aside his prejudices against motorcycle hooligans like you.

For women the situation is somewhat different. Younger women can get away with anything, with the possible exception of semi-nudity. My advice to older women, however, is to avoid net stockings, sloppy hats, gigantic pocketbooks, and the like, especially in combination with one another. It is my fervent conviction, albeit on the ridiculously narrow basis, that there is an equation in the judicial mind that says "kooky dress = kooky broad" that applies to more mature women. Why this should be so, I can only speculate. Perhaps the judges have all read their Sartre and are convinced of his concept of "*les quarante manies*"—the madness of the Forties. Perhaps it's just that they feel threatened by any intrusion of female ego by someone of approximately their own age into the cocoon of the male-dominant female-subservient courthouse atmosphere. Perhaps they are justified by experience. All I know is that women in floppy hats tend to lose. If I were female, and a bit older, I would stick to basic blue and sensible shoes. The Julie look, rather than the Tricia look, and avoid Zazu Pitts at all costs.

How old is older? Well, if they have stopped calling you miss and started calling you madam, I'm afraid you have passed the great divide.

CHAPTER III

TWIXT SUMMONS AND TRIAL: SETTLEMENT OFFERS, LAWYERS, AND WHAT TO DO ABOUT THEM

One thing about filing a lawsuit: it's an almost infallible method of getting the other side's attention. Before that summons arrived, you may have been just a pesky voice on the other end of the telephone or a presence in the In-Box. But now at the very least, you are a nagging storm cloud on the horizon, presaging a time-consuming trip down to the courthouse by the defendant or a lawyer he must pay (in some jurisdictions, corporations *must* be represented by attorneys in Small Claims Court), plus some potential negative advertising if the defendant is a business. In addition they will probably lose and have to pay you your money anyway, plus the cost of filing, service, and other court fees.

If you have to sue chances are that's the last you'll hear from the other side until trial, unless a lawyer gets involved; in that case you'll probably get a settlement offer if he thinks you have any sort of case.

It's difficult to generalize about when to settle. In many cases, depending on how pressed you are for time and whether you think you can win in front of the judge, you may find it better to accept a reasonable compromise and be done with the matter. After all, the object of the game is not to sue but to achieve reasonable satisfaction. At other times, you may not want to take a penny less than you believe the trip to the courthouse will get you.

The context of settlement offers is as good a place as any to talk about the influence of a lawyer on the Small Claims process.

Let's take it from the top and consider what it is that lawyers do all day.

Most people seem to think of a lawyer mostly as a sort of walking rule book, someone who can tell you what the law "is." This is somewhat like looking at a mathematician as repository of the multiplication tables. A lawyer is much more than just a master or a looker-up of rules. He is an advocate, a person whose job it is to persuade the court that the rules fit the facts of the case in a way advantageous to his client. Legal education is designed to impart skills in the intricate process of weaving the tangled threads of:

- Statutes, that is the laws "on the books."
- Legal "precedent," decided cases that shed light on how these laws should be brought to bear on differing legal circumstances.
- Sundry unclassifiable legal principles and rules of thumb.
- What can be made of the "facts" of a client's case, which can be used in his favor.

These are the "substantive" legal variables involved in this process.

When you add to them the complicating fillip of a vast body of procedural and evidentiary rules prescribing the way in which you may, must, and mustn't argue your case, perhaps it becomes less mysterious to you how it is that good lawyers can argue almost infinitely about almost anything.

This skill of being an intellectual Palladin can be used to shoot down injustice in anomalous legal circumstances or to annihilate the spirit of a thousand laws in the service of interests that most reasonable men would agree to be downright evil without so much as smudging a municipal ordinance.

Both are done every day as part and parcel of the so-called "adversary system" whose philosophy underlies all our legal process. As you know, under the adversary system, each "side" tries simultaneously to build up its case and tear down the other side's, all in the hope that somehow the truth will out. It assumes equally matched opponents with equal resources are contending, and a number of other conditions that may or may not exist in real life. Its actual workings have always brought to my mind Winston Churchill's description of Democracy as "the worst possible system except for all the others."

Maybe the above mini-exegesis on lawyers will explain the somewhat contemptuous perspective in which a good lawsmith holds the "rule book" aspect of the law. He knows that this so-called "black letter law" is not the answer, but the starting point. In the first place language is an imperfect instrument and almost always ambiguous. In the second, even if he is faced with an iron-clad rule directly against him, he can still always argue the other side, on the grounds, for example, that the underlying *purpose* of the law would not be served by applying it in this instance.

(Perhaps this discussion will also explain why it is so difficult to get a straight answer out of a lawyer on anything. There virtually are no straight answers, despite all the laws and all the precedents, since upon analysis, seemingly slight variations in circumstances can lead to opposite results in otherwise similar situations.)

What this means for you is that if the other side has a lawyer, there's some good news and some bad news.

The good news will come later at the trial. Then, if you are representing yourself against a lawyer, the judge will tend to act as yours, particularly if the other side is trying to rely on fairly technical points of law, or is foolish enough to badger you in any way in the courtroom.

This tendency really does present a significant advantage for you. The judge is an American. He roots for underdogs. Any number of times, I've seen an attorney finish an argument with a judge that certainly sounded technically formidable to me, and have the judge answer something to the effect of, "Well now, counselor, that may be true, but don't you think . . ." and there would follow some fairly thin legal grounds on which the judge could base a recovery for the other side. Sometimes a lawyer can argue his way out of it, sometimes he can't. (Some judges are rather fond of their own legal pronounciomentos, even completely spontaneous ones, and strongly resist efforts to undermine them; others are more open-minded and will "buy" a good counter-argument.) But when the judge refers to the other side as "counselor" you know he's in your corner, at that particular moment at least.

Meanwhile, however, you are going to have to live with the bad news, which is that you are dealing with a pro.

1. Even though, if you read on, you will not be facing negotiations with a completely empty quiver, the lawyer is going to be more experienced and adept at such horse-trading than you. It's not that he's going to suddenly talk you into signing away the homestead, but he will probably move to make settling at his price sound like a very reasonable course of action (which it may well be).

2. His very presence in court tends to keep the judge more hemmed in to the legal straight-and-narrow. If there is some technical point of law which defeats your case, a judge would be more likely to overlook or ignore it or to make a compromise settlement (which at least gives you *something*) if there is no lawyer there.

Having the lawyer present, however, changes the situation considerably; with a "brother" at the bar present, the judge is no longer the sole repository of the law, or the only participant in the trial who is not somewhat overawed by the legal setting. He is necessarily inhibited to some extent in playing the game of genial Big Daddy and is pushed to a more normally formalistic view of the law. In theory, this cuts both ways, since you may have technicalities on your side too. But the other side's lawyer is not about to point that out, and the judge may not realize it, even though he will be filling in as your lawyer to some extent.

If you are really in the right, it probably won't end up making that much difference whether the other side has a whole platoon of lawyers or not.

3. The lawyer's presence in the case will lead the judge to wonder why the case was not settled. The judge knows that a good lawyer will always try to settle, par-

ticularly a small case; and will assume some sort of offer was made and rejected.

In real life, some 80 percent or 90 percent of suits filed are settled before they reach the trial. This conserves considerable judicial time and energy (and thus tax money), and so judges are always glad to see that the case is settled. This argument applies even more to Small Claims Court, where the stakes are lower.

In a situation like this, the judge will be asking himself why you wouldn't settle. Was the offer too low, or were you just unreasonable? If you were unreasonable then, were you the same all the way along the line, and hence less deserving of getting any judicial "breaks" that could be slipped in?

So, if you are there and the other side has a lawyer, I think you are starting off with something of a shadow strike against you. The judge I believe starts out with a "I-hope-we're-not-just-wasting-our-time-here-on-a-petty-matter-that-should-have-been-settled" feeling.

Occasionally, a judge will even break into a presentation and ask (the lawyer usually): "Why wasn't this case settled, counselor?" It's getting a little ahead of ourselves, but you should be prepared to answer that question yourself, particularly after a lawyer tells the judge that he made an offer and it was refused.

Just a statement like, "Well, I know coming to court costs the public time and money, but I didn't feel that the $65 was fair settlement. Of course you're the one who has to decide what is." Once again, the object of the game is to give the judge an impression of reasonableness, even if you are the most stubborn s.o.b. on the block. Unless your demeanor shows you to be a completely pigheaded person, just a few words can probably dispel the judge's doubts. If the judge doesn't bring the subject up, however, you should not mention it.

4. Finally, the lawyer may be an "Arnie," our old friend from New York City with the killer instinct, and he will try to delay or trick you. Some of these situations we've already dealt with. Others will be considered later.

So, the phone rings and the voice on the other side introduces itself as Joe Lawyer from Dewey, Cheatum, and Howe. He is well-spoken, tells you he has called about your suit, and perhaps asks you what happened. Somewhere, along the line, he slides in a hint that he might just be willing to settle. He might just pass the question, "Well I'll tell you, you have a certain amount of right on your side. If you want to save some time, I might be able to persuade Mr. Client to . . ." or he might lead up to it, more slowly, feeling you out: "Are you sure you want to carry this all the way to court?"

Generally the offer you receive will be carapaced with a certain amount of huffing and puffing, containing equal elements of contriteness and intimidation. On one hand, there will be ingratiating apologies for the amount of inconvenience caused by the whole "misunderstanding." On the other, there are apt to be dire insinuations that you don't have a legal leg to stand on and that no court of law could possibly find in your favor. (One often-used ploy is to try to convince you that the law makes the buyer bear the burden of proof that the machine was used according to directions. This is baloney.) At any rate, you will be reassured that the outfit wants to do the right thing and preserve its sterling reputation even though it knows it can win, that everybody's time is too valuable to waste on court, that you seem like a reasonable person who realizes all this, and how about calling it even for X dollars.

The thing to remember at this point is that you are pretty much in the driver's seat. There is usually very little reason to settle for less than 70 percent of your legitimate claim. If you have a good case, you have a reasonably good chance of getting 100 percent by just trotting on down there. (If the offer is being made just before the trial down at the courthouse, you have even less reason to give up anything; a bird in the hand may generally be worth two in the bush; but your fingers happen to be pretty close to the bush at that particular moment.)

Why give up anything at all? First of all, you will

avoid whatever slight risk there is that you will lose your case. Secondly, it's nicer to get the money faster, even if there isn't quite as much of it. You have, after all, made your point.

Also don't forget the human element in all this. A lawyer has to show his client that he gave him *something* for the fee he is going to lay out. At the least, he's going to try a little bit harder to beat you in court. Indeed, if you really aggravate him, it's possible that the lawyer will transfer the case to regular court or appeal the decision, just out of good old spite and the incentive to impress his client that he is giving the other side a rough time. Put yourself in the other side's shoes. For the client, it might just be worth the slight extra cost to make you cool your heels for a year before the case comes to trial. You might not even contest the case after all that time for one reason or another, and you will have to go to the expense of hiring a lawyer, just like he did. Very tempting. And, believe it or not, lawyers have egos too, and don't like to have their plumage ruffled.

Given these considerations, you might wonder why such transfer or appeal, which would negate the entire usefulness of Small Claims Court, is not automatic, standard operating procedure for the other side's lawyer. There are several reasons. First of all, it costs some money, and its equivalent, time. Even the lowliest shyster usually has bigger fish to fry. But also, such practices are likely to arouse the ire of the judge. Justice may be blind, but judges are not. They get to know the assorted cast of lawyers who come before them pleading their various causes. Judges generally have a warm place in their hearts for Small Claims Court and they don't like to see plaintiffs deprived of the forum by some smart-aleck fast shuffle. If this smarty pants goes around playing too many games like this, the judge consciously or unconsciously will keep this in mind in ruling on his motions, giving him the benefit of the doubt, or any of the other many important discretionary decisions the judge makes during a trial.

Lawyers often skip steps and make technical booboos

which judges generally ignore in the interests of reasonable justice. Stringent application of the rules to everything a lawyer does can have a nasty effect on his batting average, paperwork, and digestion. Although in negotiating with you, the lawyer realizes he has the power to give you a rough time by playing cute, he knows if he does too much of it, the judge can and will do the same to him. The situation is still balanced in your direction.

In short, there's no dishonor in settling and it is usually worth giving up a little in the interests of saving yours and the court's time; and seventy-five one-hundredths of a bird in the hand is probably a reasonable estimate of the present value of one in the bush.

If you agree in principle to a settlement, the next thing is to get the cash. If you are dealing with a lawyer over the phone a few days before the trial, ask him when you get your money. His answer will probably be an unspecific "in a few days" or something of the sort. At this point, he probably isn't sure himself since he has to call his client and tell him to send a check.

Your answer should be, "Fine, as long as it gets here before the court date." If he doesn't want to guarantee that, then ask him what assurance you have that you will in fact get the money. He will reassure you there is no problem. Then you should say, "Okay, if you put that in writing, you've got yourself a deal," and tell him if you get a letter before the trial stipulating the terms of the settlement (amount and when you are going to get it), you will be happy to call it a bargain.

The way the other side reacts to this proposal is a pretty good indication of whether or not they can be trusted to honor the deal. After all, this is merely a statement of what you have already agreed to. If they intend to keep their word, what possible objection can there be to having everything down in black and white? You can explain in response to any manifestations of injury and disappointment at your lack of faith in handshakes that, well, that's not really it, but it will just make you feel a lot better. Personally, if the other side won't put its word in writing, I wouldn't drop the suit.

Ninety-nine times out of a hundred, he will agree to this afterall perfectly reasonable request. If he doesn't, or the check doesn't show up, prepare to meet him in court.

Having this agreement in some cases can be better than an actual court judgment from your point of view. First of all, it constitutes a legally binding contract perfectly enforceable in court, but precludes the case from being heard on its merits. That is, you have a piece of paper that entitles you to your money even if your original claim was invalid. You agreed to accept a certain amount of money in exchange for forgoing the right to press your claim in court at that time. You performed your part of the bargain by not suing at the time. Now the court is going to make the other side perform his commitment irrespective of the merits of your original claim. On the other hand, you still have the option of going ahead with the suit again if he doesn't pay.

Incidentally, if you think you are really dealing with a scoundrel, it would be good to demand a clause that says:

> In the event of his default on this agreement, Mr. X agreed to pay the cost of collection, including reasonable attorney's fees.

That way, if something goes wrong, all you do is call up a lawyer, put the matter in his hands, and let the other side worry about paying his fees.

The same general principles apply if you are settling down at the courtroom before trial.

> Get the agreement in writing. The writing should stipulate: (1) the reason for the payment—"settlement of Small Claims Court Action No. ————, Third District Court"; (2) amount to be paid;

(3) time for payment; (4) stipulation of defendant bearing collection costs upon default.

Here is an example of such an agreement:

It is hereby agreed by the undersigned parties (you), Plaintiff and (XYZ Co.), defendant in the action of (you) vs. (XYZ Co.), Docket No. ————, 197—— in (court) that the above entitled action is to be settled without trial for the sum of $XX to be received by plaintiff from defendant by (date). It is also agreed that plaintiff shall notify the court of this settlement and discontinue the above action.

In the event of default upon this agreement, plaintiff shall have the right to collect the above sum, in addition to Court Costs and the reasonable cost of collection, including reasonable attorney's fees.

Incidentally, some Small Claims Courts have forms for settling that you can use, but they usually don't have collection cost payment provision. Just write one in and have the other side initial it.

If the other side absolutely balks at the attorney's fee provision, you don't need it. You can always sue again in Small Claims Court based on the agreement. All it will really cost you is an extra trip to the courthouse to get a summons issued. (The filing and service fees associated with this new suit will be added to your judgment, as usual; but you should add the court costs of your original suit to what you are asking for in the new one.) But you should ask yourself why they are so reluctant, particularly if you are willing to give them ample time to pay. As far as informing the court of the settlement, telephone them and ask them what you have to do. Sometimes the telephone call itself will suffice. Other courts may require a letter from you.

If you fail to reach a settlement or don't get an offer in the first place, then you'll see 'em in court. Now, if you are dealing with an Arnie-type, you had better be prepared for more delaying tactics. The one that is left is a request for a continuance down at the courtroom. Any old-baloney excuse is often good enough.

You will vastly increase your chances of beating a motion for continuance if you lay your groundwork correctly. Try the following letter, a copy of which you can show to the judge:

Dear (other side),

I regret that our mutual attempt at resolving the matter of my defective motorcycle did not succeed. At least we tried, and the matter will be resolved at our trial (date).

Or, if there has been no settlement attempt:

As you know from being served with summons, our disagreement over the terms of the motorcycle warranty will be resolved in court on (date).

It occurs to me that it is possible this date may be inconvenient for you. I would be delighted to agree to a continuance

(any Thursday next month)
(to the week of the 5th)
(... etc ...)

if you give me 72 hours notice to reschedule my time off from work. You can (contact me every day at ————) or (leave a message at ————).

Otherwise, I trust the matter will be settled on the 22nd.

Sincerely,

He can't say he wasn't warned.

CHAPTER IV

AT THE COURT

When you arrive for the trial, you're going to see a scene that looks like a cross between the money changers in the Temple and Gimbel's basement on Washington's Birthday Sale. Quite a cross-section of America will usually be gathered together in the Halls of Justice, and if you are any kind of people-watcher, the inevitable fifteen or twenty minutes that pass before anything gets going will do so quickly. What you'll be witnessing is the real commerce of the courthouse, lawyers dashing to file papers, huddled last minute settlements being struck, clerks gearing up for the coming session.

Also, this is a good opportunity to run through your case one last time, since the courtroom show will probably be interesting enough to rivet your attention no matter how nervous you are.

CHECKING THE CALENDAR—IF YOU ARE ON THE MOTION LIST

One optional pre-courtroom item of business is to make sure you're on the list for that day or evening. You can do this by checking the "calendar," if you can find it. If you're lucky, it will be on the wall outside the courtroom or on the desk in the clerk's office. Often it's just in the clerk's inside breast pocket and you'll have to wait until you get in the courtroom and the list is called. If by some chance you are not on it, tell the clerk. If you find out you are not on it after he has called the list in court, you should feel free to walk up and tell him, even if something else is going on. Lawyers do it all the time and don't get bitten.

If you do check the calendar, see whether it is divided up into the "case" list and the "motion" list. If you are on the case list, your case will actually be tried that day. If you find yourself on the motion list, however, it almost certainly means that the other side is going to make a motion for continuance. (Sometimes, you will have been warned by the court of this in advance, sometimes not.) If you expected this maneuver and laid your groundwork via letter as suggested, you stand a good fighting chance of beating the continuance.

Even if you haven't done so, however, prepare to argue against it. When the lawyer gives his excuse, ask him why it was not possible for him to reach you. If he says he tried to call you, ask him when. When he answers, you might mention how peculiar it is that your phone did not ring, since you were home at the time. You might mention that the U.S. Mail is not that slow, either, if his excuse is such that he had a few days notice. Telegrams also exist, and can be sent by phone.

If you happen to be missing work that day, a good technique is to turn to the judge and say something like the following: "Well, your honor, I would have had no objection if I had been told in advance, but now I've had to miss some work and I'm going to have to miss some more work if I can even get the time off to come down here again. I think I should be allowed to add the wages I missed to the amount that I'm suing for. I'm ready to go right now. I was home last night, I was home the night before, I was home this morning, and there were plenty of chances to get in touch with me and save this lost time. If he really wanted to save me the trouble of coming down here—where there's a will, there's a way. So, I really feel that it's very unfair to ask for a delay. I'd like to get this thing over with, but I'll agree to it if we change the suit to include XX dollars for the money I'm going to lose for having to come down here one more time."

The judge is not going to buy this argument, since

that isn't the way things are done. The real reason you are making it is to cast as heavy a burden as possible on the other side to justify their request.

You want to express your restrained, justifiable outrage at this tactic. Nine times out of ten, the lawyer really could have contacted you, had he taken the trouble. And in 90 percent of the remaining 10 percent of the time, his excuse is lousy, anyway.

What you are up against is custom. Lawyers are, in fact, busy people and are constantly rearranging their schedules. As a matter of professional courtesy, they tend to acquiesce to a request for a continuance from the other side. And, even if there is some grumbling, the judge is inclined to "give every dog one bite," that is, to grant the first request for continuance automatically.

These habits carry over into Small Claims Court. But the big difference is that lawyers who want a continuance in a regular case will almost always notify the other side. Somehow when the other side is a civilian, it's not as important.

If you don't make the point that it's important to you, no one else is about to, so speak up. Showing the judge a copy of the letter you wrote requesting notice of continuance should really drive the spike in.

At this point, the judge will at least be aware that you have an objection to the continuance being granted. If he thinks the other side's excuse is good enough, he may just make a few placatory remarks to you and grant it. Or, he might suggest you reconsider settling.

More likely, he will turn to the other side and say, "Well, what do you feel about that, counselor?" or something of the sort. A lawyer will usually start to babble about continuances being the unavoidable breaks in the game of Justice, or something like that, and reiterate his excuses. (Don't interrupt him.)

At this point, the judge is almost surely going to make a comment that indicates which way he is leaning. He has a number of choices. He can hold the trial now and tell the lawyer he can speak for his client. Or he can grant the continuance. Or there is a third option, which you should suggest to him if he indicates he is leaning toward continuance. You should ask him to enter a default judgment in your favor, thus putting the burden on the other side to come down to the court and make a motion for a new trial.

As you will see, this motion will be something you can probably deal with by mail. Hence, you make the other side waste a trip down, then you both come down again. The score will be three trips for the lawyer, two for your opponent, and two for you, so at least you will be ahead in the spite column.

At this point, even if you've been shot down on the specific request for a continuance, you've put the lawyer through a couple of paces and just perhaps implanted a seed in the judge's brain that maybe he shouldn't be granting continuances so freely in Small Claims Court cases.

IF THE OTHER SIDE DOESN'T SHOW— DEFAULT JUDGMENTS AND MOTIONS TO VACATE

If the other side doesn't show up, you will win by default. Usually, the "default judgment" will be entered automatically, but not become final for a week or two. This is to give the other side one more chance. The law, based as it is on the "adversary system," frowns on default judgments. No one can ever be absolutely sure that summons was delivered, the case was not frivolous, or the damages not exaggerated.

Getting a default judgment may well not be the end of the matter; if the other side wants to come down and make a motion to "vacate" the judgment, they will probably get a new trial.

If you are notified in a few days that you must appear in court to answer a motion to vacate, the question for you is whether you have to go down that day. If you do, what will probably happen is that the judge will probably decide he might as well try the case on its merits as long as everyone is there.

If you can, it is much better to write a letter to the court saying that you oppose the motion because of the hardship to you of getting to the court once again, losing work, and wages. Although technically the judge is not supposed to go into the merits of the case, you might briefly outline the salient facts and include xeroxes of any correspondence or documents. Stress any delaying tactics the other side has used.

Probably the judge is going to grant the motion no matter what you do, but you have at least a chance of avoiding a trip to the court this way.

Now since you've technically been summoned to court yourself to answer this motion, you may have a few doubts about blithely not showing up. Well, you weren't told to come for a new trial, you were told to come for a motion for a new trial. There are different kinds of legal "appearances," each appropriate for certain situations. You could have appeared "by attorney," for example; and there's no violation of the spirit of that particular summons in appearing in the form of a written answer. The best thing to do is send a cover letter to the Clerk along with your letter to the judge. The cover letter should say that you do not think you can make it, but hope the enclosed letter to the judge will constitute a sufficient appearance for the purposes of the motion. You might also indicate which trial dates might be convenient to you in case the judge grants the motion. Ask and you might receive.

IF THERE IS AN ARBITRATION OPTION

If you're in New York City or another jurisdiction that has an optional arbitration system, the first thing the clerk will do in the courtroom is read a statement that tells you you have a choice of going before the judge or an arbitrator. Sometimes the statement will provide that when your name is called you go to an arbitrator unless you specifically state that you want to appear before the judge. That is the case in New York

City, for example, which also provides that there is no appeal from an arbitration award.

To arbitrate or not to arbitrate? Studies made in New York City have concluded that arbitrators are "somewhat more prone to compromise" than judges. This means that more people get something, but fewer get what they ask for. An arbitrator is less likely to give you out-of-pocket expenses, for example. On the other hand, my personal belief is that if the other side has a lawyer, you may be better off to choose a judge if the arbitrator is in fact a volunteer lawyer. This is because I think that a lawyer is less subconsciously prepared to find completely against a brother lawyer than a judge is. To a judge, a lawyer is just another one of those whining pests who keep asking him to decide things. He is likely to be much more willing to say in effect, "You lose, now scram," than is a lawyer.

If the other side is just another John Q. Citizen, by all means use the arbitrator and save everyone time.

Otherwise, my irrational, prejudiced, but quite stubborn instinct says use the judge. It's your decision—and your right.

CHAPTER V

AT TRIAL

As you observe the proceedings you will see that each new trial consists of several steps. First the case is called and the parties approach the bench. In some places the clerk now characterizes the dispute for the judge in a sentence or two. The plaintiff is asked to tell his or her side of the story. During the presentation the judge may or may not ask questions. At the end, he turns to the defendant and asks either whether the defendant wishes to cross-examine, or merely requests that side of the story. (If a lawyer is there, there will probably be cross-examination, if for no other reason than to allow the lawyer to give the client the feeling that the fee is being earned.) After the defendant has spoken and possibly been cross-examined in turn, the judge will probably ask a few questions of his own, as well as make various comments.

After the judge has satisfied himself that he pretty well understands the issues of the case, he may either announce his decision right there, or "reserve" it. (Many judges reserve all decisions because they feel that SCC plaintiffs get too excited if they lose, which some indeed do.) What's left to happen is the mailing of a postcard by the clerk announcing the decision and the amount of the judgment, if any.

All right, you've been sitting there watching the cases go by, heart slightly aflutter between each case as the clerk prepares to call the next one. All of a sudden you hear your name called. Mouth suddenly just a bit dry, you stand and walk to the bench, discovering just how long a few steps can be. In an instant, you are sworn in and the judge looks down, asking you to tell your story.

Well, from here on in you are flying solo. No one can write your lines for you. Perhaps the best preparation is for us right now to talk about what a judge does all day. When His Honor presides over a trial, he has several jobs.

First, he referees the proceedings, supervising the examination of witnesses, deciding what evidence should be admitted and what the Rules of Evidence dictate should not be heard.

Next, he oversees the jury, when there is one, in its determination of facts, and serves as fact determiner when there isn't.

Finally, he "lays down the law," that is, he determines what rules of law apply to facts, and interprets how they shall be applied and what the result is.

Now, he doesn't do any of these things according to what he personally feels is fair this particular day, or at least he isn't supposed to. In a regular trial, there are all sorts of restraints on a judge, all sorts of abstract but detailed standards by which he is supposed to reach a decision. These standards relate to the kind and amount of evidence necessary to "prove" a "fact"; to the manner in which the proceedings are conducted; and to all sorts of "technicalities" quite important to your case.

These standards are far too convoluted to bother with here. Believe me, you really aren't going to miss out on one of life's essential experiences by avoiding an exhaustive examination of whether disbelief of a denial will defeat a presumption by supporting an inference of the existence of the denied fact, and the rest of the stuff all those angels sitting on the heads of all those pins talk about. It's all a kaleidoscope of over-refined gobbledygook designed to accommodate decisions reached on fundamental notions of fair play. Yet, these are the rules by which the courtroom game is played, and one of the big jobs of a lawyer in a trial is to safeguard a client's rights by making sure the judge sticks to these rules.

Another job is to help educate the judge on exactly what law should be applied to the situation. The "law" is millions and millions of pages of statutes, cases, defining how they should be interpreted, commentaries, rules, regulations, and principles. No human being could ever hope to absorb even a thousandth of a percent of it all. What makes it all manageable is thousands of other pages of material attempting to index it all and give a starting point to those who would determine what "law" should be applied to any factual situation. "Advocacy" means sifting through this chaff and interpreting it in a way favorable to one's side of the case. This is what lawyers' "briefs" submitted by both sides and commented on by the judge's clerk are all about. The educational value to the judge of that sort of input is a fundamental to every trial, and what runs up million dollar legal fees.

Small Claims Court, however, is high-volume, low-overhead, bargain basement (in the money sense) justice. Here there are no briefs or law clerks to help sharpen the issues, although a $200 case can be just as complex as the $20 million lawsuit that produces tens of thousands of pages of briefs, testimony and argument and takes years to resolve. Nor, for practical purposes in the majority of cases, is there the threat of appeal to a higher court if the judge gets too far out of line. In short, for better or worse (and it's generally the former, as far as I'm concerned), there simply is no time for the painstaking inquiry into the facts and debate over law that is provided for in a regular trial. We are talking about a system in which the average case takes about five minutes. Compared with the amount of time expended on normal cases, this is a mere split second of judicial time. In this time, a judge must make his best estimate of the facts, apply the relevant law, and reach a decision as to how much, if anything, the plaintiff should get. Given a job like this, one cannot realistically expect adherence to abstract decision-making standards. The purpose is swift reckoning, and that's the result.

So what it all adds up to is that in Small Claims

Court, more than in any other legal forum, getting the judge on your side is the be-all of the exercise. The judge is the man who tells it like it's gonna be, and he can call the shots any old way he happens to see them. You will be trying to present yourself and your cause in a way that makes the right thing happen in that complicated decision machine between his ears.

Now, not even the good Dr. Freud could tell you everything that His Honor takes into account in reaching his decision, and to what degree legal training versus toilet training is the scale-tipper in any given case.

But almost all judges tend to relax their usual formal decision-making standards when acting in their Small Claims Court roles. They consider themselves freer to exercise a sort of judicial X-ray vision and inject their instinct into the fact determining process, sizing up the situation "on the whole" and making a more subjective decision than they otherwise would. Small Claims Court is a place where legalisms tend to be overshadowed by fundamental notions of what's "right."

Therefore, although it is a matter of degree, in Small Claims Court, much more than in a regular courtroom, one is appealing to the "heart" of the judge, that is to his emotions, his prejudices, his whims.

It should be made perfectly clear at this point that there are a lot of things the last statement does not mean.

It does not mean that the way to win is to cozy up to the judge and try to make him like you, or to go into the court with a tear in your eye, a trembling lower lip, and a heart-rending tale of the iniquitous behavior of the nasty old other side.

The judge's heart doesn't rend that easily. Imagine this guy's day-to-day life. He sits looking down (figuratively and literally) at this flow of human woes that society sends him to resolve, or at least dispose of. Rogues who would cut your fingers off to get at the rings, accident victims moaning about their pain and suffering, messy divorces, deadbeats, saints, and sinners —you name them, he has to settle their quarrels and their fates. This is a man who (if he has criminal court duties) has to send people to jail for half their remaining lives, who tells X to pay Y money, knowing that X will have to sell his house to do so; in short, a man who every day of his life is charged with the responsibility of making decisions that profoundly affect the lives of the people concerned.

What results from this experience is a pretty good working insight into the various goods and evils that lurk in the hearts of men. Being lied to just about every day also produces a certain skepticism in their viewpoints. The judge has heard it all before, brother. In some judges, the heavy responsibility produces what is best termed genuine wisdom; in others, all that goes into their heads is the power, and they turn into callous autocrats.

But in all of them, I think it's fair to say, this experience yields above all a certain detachment. The world of the judicial mind is at its base a very cool one, in the last analysis—clinical, aloof, and tough.

This certainly does not mean that judges cannot be the warm and compassionate human beings many of them are in private. But in their professional roles, they are of necessity hardened to making hard choices in difficult situations. Somebody wins, somebody loses. The judge decides. The judge is not, like the policeman of the motto, your friend. He is your judge and you should have no contrary illusions.

Another thing to get straight is the role of the judge's own private prejudices. As far as I have been able to see, plaintiffs get even-handed treatment irrespective of race, sex, religion, creed, national origin, length of hair, sexual orientation, or any of the other identities that the words "prejudice" or "discrimination" call to mind. Armenians, broads, butches, beggars, chinks, commies, Democrats, drag queens, eggheads, fags, fats, fems, freaks, frogs, gooks, goys, hardhats, hippies, kanucks, kikes, krouts, mackerel snappers, mexies, micks, nazis, niggers, nips, okies, out-of-staters, polaks, portagees, redskins, Republicans, spics, squares, students, Transylvanians, ukes, wasps, wops, and any other U.S. citizens coming into court to assert their rights can do so in any of the courts that I've seen in confidence that their case will be fairly considered.

If the judge has any systematic bias at all, it would seem to be pro-plaintiff. Statistically, if nothing else, you are already considerably more than half-way home the minute you walk into the door. (Indeed, J.P., the initials for "Justice of the Peace," the magistrates who still preside over these courts in many parts of the country, have traditionally only half-jokingly been said to stand for "judgment for the plaintiff."

No, I don't think anyone starts out on the wrong side of the judge. You have to get there on your own.

And, I must say over and over again, in Small Claims Courts all over this land of ours, I have been amazed at the creative efforts some people seem to put snatching defeat from the bosom of victory, persuading the judge that they should be thrown out of court. It's like going down to the police station to complain about a crime and ending up being arrested for it.

Now, Justice in Small Claims Court is about as blind as a cat on a windowsill overlooking a treeful of sparrows. In the few minutes it can allot to your case, Justice is at some level of brain function, avidly scanning for every little clue it can get. On one hand, the mind of the judge is turning the facts over and trying to fit them into this or that legal pigeonhole: figuring out what "law" applies; on the other hand, the heart of the judge is pigeonholing you. Your manner, your demeanor, your way of talking, the way you look, they are all testifying for you or against you whether your mouth is open or shut. It's all rather like pop-media-oracle Marshall McLuhan says, "The medium is the message."

Here then are several ways to get on the wrong side of the judge:

1. *Be a Nut.* A lot of nuts seem to end up suing in Small Claims Courts. They always lose. What happens is that they usually come in and put on some kind of courageous act. Danger signal number one is the

way they tell their story, rambling along in a long-winded, disjointed manner, throwing in all sorts of irrelevant details that make it obvious to the judge that, like most lonely people, what they want more than anything else is a little sympathetic attention. That they usually get, but no more. After being reminded two or three times by the judge to stick to the facts, they'll finally finish a two-minute story after about seven or eight minutes. Even at this point, it would not be too late for the nuts, were they only content to keep their mouths shut from then on. But they also cannot resist broadcasting danger signal number two and interrupting the other side as it attempts to present its case.

At this juncture, the judge's patience is beginning to fray, but he usually merely asks the saints above to give him strength and tells the offender to not interrupt please. At this point, the nut will usually provide the maraschino cherry to the impression he or she is creating by resorting to calling the other side a liar in a loud voice, or crying, or gesticulating at the slightest hint that the judge by his questions even deigns to assume for the sake of argument that anything whatsoever the evil villain on the other side said is true. At this point, the judge will usually stop the proceedings and say, "Well, I've heard what I need, you'll hear from the court about its decision."

I've seen this kind of behavior blow what I thought were really valid cases. I remember one particularly pathetic instance involving an elderly lady who was suing a dentist who had made some false teeth that were apparently very uncomfortable. I had seen this dentist sued in the same court for the same reason a couple of weeks before and lose his case. Apparently the guy needed a little more practice with his false teeth business.

However, this woman, by wailing and moaning and just making it impossible to conduct the proceedings, ended up losing against the probably incompetent dentist, who just sat there and appeared to be a respectable middle-class person. There was over $300 involved, a large sum for that lady, and legally, she probably deserved it; but by being so hard to deal with in court, she made the judge think that she had been hard to deal with as a customer and he did not probe into any facts of the case that might have helped her.

Of course, we all know *you're* not a nut. Therefore: (1) Do yourself, the judge, the clerk, and everyone else in the courtroom who has to sit through your story a favor. Make it short and sweet. Succinctness and organization are qualities highly appreciated by the judge as indicia of reasonableness, intelligence, and other qualities which speak for your worthiness to collect. Stick to the facts, the relevant facts, the relevant facts being those facts which help you establish the "elements" of your case. (You will hear more about "elements" later.) Do not belabor with operatic wails and laments the details of the outrages the other side has visited upon you. If you've been given a run-around, you can score the maximum number of points by just alluding to it statistically and manifesting a philosophical air: "Well, I called them three times, wrote them two letters, which I brought, and made two trips, then gave up." (If you are an incorrigible thespian, you can always shrug slightly here. *Slightly*.) If the judge wants to hear more, he'll ask you.

I remember one man who after a long boring harangue against the other side thrust a letter at the judge, saying, "And, Your Honor, may I show you this insulting letter they sent me?" The judge in a wonderfully world-weary tone said, "Show me the insulting letter." When he had read it, he handed it back, answering, "Sorry, I'm not sure who's insulting who," which took a little wind out of the plaintiff's sails.

(2) *Don't interrupt or call the other side a liar.* The guy may be lying through his teeth, he may be slandering your sainted mother, or worse, he may be scoring points; but if you break in with a dramatic shout of "That's a lie!" as many people do, and make no mistake, you will be tempted to do so, you are hurting yourself. It's immature, and it puts the judge in the bad position of implicitly calling him a liar if he rules in

your favor. Not even judges like to do that sort of thing, so he might on a close case be inclined to give the benefit of the doubt as opposed to the "accuser." Experienced trial lawyers love to provoke adverse witnesses into calling another witness a liar. It loses points with the jury like crazy for that witness. It doesn't gain any with judges for you.

If you do want to set the record straight on something your opponent has said, just preface your remarks with a gentle "Well, I remember what Mr. X said about Y a little differently . . ."

If you want to you could even go up there with a little pad, and every time he says something you think is wrong, jot down a key word. Then when it's your turn again, just refer to the notes. This will have the psychological value of letting the judge know you thought he was lying two or three times, or whatever the number of the words you have on the note pad.

2. *Be a Perry Mason.* Perry Masonitis is a disease of the male. It seems to be closely correlated with a surfeit of self-righteousness and a deficient sense of humor. Persons afflicted by this syndrome, believe that, by God, they're the universally acknowledged PTA debate champion, they're as smart as any lawyer, they can get up there and do that stuff, and they're going to show that shyster on the other side a thing or two. Not only the law, but God, Yale, Truth, Justice, the United States Constitution, and the principles of self-determination are on their side. Reason, too, so why should they listen to any compromise? Never!!

What these turkeys don't realize is that they are not only being obnoxious, not only making idiots out of themselves, but depriving themselves of a sort of "amateur status" which accrues to Small Claims Court plaintiffs. Because you are a layman and unfamiliar with the arcane mysteries of the law, you gain the benefit of a certain indulgence by the judge, a willingness to overlook the technicalities and try to do "substantial justice."

But when you start acting like a lawyer, the tendency

for the judge is to hold you to the standards of a lawyer, both in terms of being more prepared to raise technicalities ("Yes, but have you read paragraph 14 of the standard lease, young man?") and not acting as his lawyer if the other side is represented. Instead, if there is a lawyer on the other side, what's going on is a little private joke between the judge and him in which the judge says, "Okay, I know what we're up against. Let's see if we can't just hoist this turkey by his own petard." Even if there is no lawyer, it is simply too tempting for the judge to show Perry Mason just how smart he is about the law, which isn't very.

This sometimes takes the form of the judge luring him into a little Socratic dialogue about the law, giving him little hypothetical examples and luring him down the intellectual garden path to a destination that old Perry suddenly realizes is not what he had in mind at all. Almost inevitably, the Perry Mason walks away with some legal education but no money.

The classic technique is to maneuver the Perry Mason into a situation where he says something is the law which really isn't. This happened to a friend of mine who tried to stick up for his rights in Traffic Court (where, of course, the same principles apply).

A recently transplanted New Jerseyan, he got stopped in Los Angeles for entering a crosswalk while a pedestrian was in it, way over on the other side of the street. Apparently the pedestrian had just stepped off the corner. Now, in Western states, the pedestrian seems to be considered an endangered species and drivers actually try to avoid hitting them. But back in the Wild East, if anyone actually drove like that, they would start a chain car collision stretching the length of Boston to Washington, and be committed to the loony bin as well. Although the more or less same traffic regulations are on the books, it is the custom neither to obey them nor to enforce them.

Well, Joe, who actually isn't the Perry Mason type at all, went into court and somehow gave the judge the wrong impression. (It may have been because he started arguing his innocence after having pleaded *"Nolo Contendere,"* which is a middle plea that says, "I don't plead guilty but I don't want to argue, so I will pay the fine.")

Anyway, Joe began to argue, trying to explain to the judge that he really was a safe driver, that there was no reason to enforce that law when the pedestrian was 70 feet away. As he tells it, "The judge kept asking me questions and twisting what I said. All of a sudden I found myself basing my whole argument on whether or not New Jersey had a law like California's." At that point, the judge offered him a choice of paying the regular $20 fine or of Double-or-Nothing, saying he would look up the New Jersey law on his lunch hour. With a vague sinking sensation, Joe took the gamble.

After lunch, the judge began court again and called him before the bench, where he had a New Jersey lawbook with a bookmark in it. Grinning evilly, as he handed Joe the book, he said "It's not nice to fool Mother Nature." Needless to say, the treasury of the State of California grew by $40.

We all know you're not a Perry Mason, or any other species of wise guy. You're too smart to set yourself up for a slap-down.

Therefore, stow the "whereupons," "consequentlys," "subsequentlys," "ensueds," "altercations," "proceededs" and the Ciceronian syntax. Stick to the good old Anglo-Saxon vulgate mother-tongue that is your customary informal mode of expression. Leave the rest to Raymond Burr.

Above all, don't start talking law at the judge. Because if you do, he's going to start talking law back to you. (There will be some exceptions to this general rule mentioned later; but these are usually special instances, and elaborate pains have been taken to show you what kind of special verbal genuflections to make to avoid the Perry Masonitis trap.)

3. *Be slow to get the hint to settle.* I have never understood why presumably intelligent people disregard the broadest hints from the judge. I remember a case

in New York, an automobile accident. This young couple was suing for destruction of their ten-year-old car in an accident. Apparently they themselves had bought it not long before for about $300. They appeared before a judge who liked to see settlements. ("Settlements are always better," he later said. "Both sides are dissatisfied but happy.") The other side appeared "by attorney," that is, the defendant did not appear in person.

The judge immediately sized up the situation for what it was, a case where the lawyer was representing an insurance company, which presumably had offered some sort of settlement rather than be dragged down to court. The couple started talking about their beautiful $300 car being destroyed, and it was obvious that it really meant a lot to these young people, so the judge cut them off and turned to the attorney: "Didn't you offer to settle with these people?" Legal shop talk translation: "What are you doing wasting my time and your time with this minor matter? We both know the insurance company will absorb anything under $100 without a peep. It's an insignificant drop in the bucket to your client and it's a big thing to these people. C'mon, be a sport, give 'em a few bucks. So the rates go up two hundred thousandths of a cent next year. We all know no-fault insurance is coming.

The lawyer answered: "Your Honor, I already offered $75, which is pretty good in a case where we have no liability. This is a situation with an uncontested left turn in front of my client." (Translation: I tried. They haven't got a legal leg to stand on. In that case, the best I could do was $75. But the jerks won't take it. What do you want me to do?)

Judge: "Well, why don't you give them $90?" Seeing that the lawyer was going to protest, he turned to the plaintiffs, saying, "You know, in view of what I've just heard, $90 might be a pretty good settlement."

Plaintiffs: (Completely missing the point) "But Your Honor, we paid $300 for the car."

Lawyer: "You see?"

Judge: "Well, I want you to go into the hall and try to reach a compromise."

Well, sure enough, they went out in the corridor, the kids wouldn't settle—they came back, had a trial—judgment for defendant.

The lesson I hope is clear. When the judge starts giving you broad hints (of any sort), he's probably doing you a favor. Why don't you take him up on it?

Most of what you have read in this chapter has dealt with how to win by not losing your case. Now a few comments directed more toward strengthening your presentation.

1. Documents and Notes

Many people are curious about whether they should go up there with notes; they're afraid they'll forget something. It turns out that very few people ever use notes, but you do see it occasionally. Suit yourself, but if you do decide you would feel more comfortable, I would limit myself to five or six key words on a three by five card, indicating the elements I want to cover in the order that I would like to cover them. And I would be as discreet as possible about using them since you are after all supposed to be giving a spontaneous recollection of the facts. If you're sitting down and you have some papers with you, some other papers, a good technique is to put everything in a file folder and clip the card outside the folder, holding the folder in your lap and glancing down at the card as needed. If you're standing up, the clip-on technique is adaptable, though a little harder unless you have some sort of table or rostrum before you.

As for documents in general, you should, of course, bring all the relevant papers with you. (It may turn out to be quite a hefty bunch, documents having a way of multiplying themselves in our mandarinized society.) Now, a huge pile of papers is going to depress the judge. He doesn't want to sort through the mess. So, if you have quite a little dossier, it's worth taking the trouble to tuck them into a file folder.

You should also have sorted them out in some relevant way. Just paper clip the ones that go together. Also, if you may have to show the judge a number of different documents—for example, a whole bunch of repair bills—it won't hurt to make up a summary sheet adding them all up. If you are organized, the judge will be favorably impressed. On the other hand, there's nothing worse than having to fish around for something up there while justice is drumming its fingers.

Also, unless you think it's really important that the judge actually see the papers, never give the judge anything unless he asks for it. Just indicate to him that you have the papers here. If he wants to see anything, he'll ask.

2. Cross-Examination

When you are through presenting your case you may be cross-examined by the other side. I really can't remember anyone ever scoring any significant points by cross-examination in Small Claims Court. There isn't enough time for all the fine-spun lawyer's traps to be woven. Anyway, if you're being cross-examined by a lawyer, he will probably ask you a number of questions, some of which may be preceded by a statement to the effect of "Isn't it true that . . ." Pause for a moment, consider the question, and if it's susceptible of a "Yes" or "No" answer, answer Yes or No.

The best weapon you have is mildness and courtesy. Don't argue, just answer the question. Don't volunteer any information beyond what is required from the question. Lawyers have lots of little tricks for making you appear to be less certain than you really are, but these are usually reserved for jury trials. And don't forget, the lawyer knows just as well as you that the judge is impatient to get on with the matter. So, if you don't answer any questions you're not sure of and you don't volunteer any extra information, you have nothing to worry about.

If your turn comes to cross-examine, what's not much use even for a skilled lawyer is probably not going to yield the Comstock lode for you. Maybe you are the universally acknowledged debating champ of Duffy's Tavern, social relations 492H, and your local PTA. Well, you might also be a good skater, but now you're working out with the Bruins. Non-lawyer cross-examinations are usually embarrassing flops. If you want to highlight a couple of points by asking one or two short questions, there's no harm in it, I suppose, but keep it short and keep it questions, not speeches.

3. After Testimony

After the testimony, the judge will probably ask a few questions of his own. If you have done a little homework on the elements of your case, you will probably see what he is driving at. And you'll be prepared to answer correctly.

This is the part of the presentation where the judge will probably be gently probing to find out if you acted reasonably. He might say, "Well, why didn't you do this?" or "Why didn't you do that?" Just tell him the truth. Because if the truth is you didn't bring the motorcycle in to have it fixed because you were so damn mad at the run-around you had gotten thus far—*say it*. And add that you didn't think that these people were going to do anything but give you more run-around, that's why you went someplace else and had it fixed. You had just had enough. And, of course, you will have two or three letters to back up your pleas of total and justifiable exasperation, having read Chapter One.

In general, this interchange after testimony is more informal, more chatty. But don't take it as an invitation to drone on forever. Take the hint from the judge; if he says, "Okay, that's enough," shut up.

Incidentally, if you're into this sort of thing, you can tell a lot about what's going on in the judge's mind from his basic body language. For example, many judges signal their decisions by reiterating a crucial fact to the losing side, then just turning their heads away. "Well, it's true that he hit you from the back, but you were changing lanes at the time, weren't you?" Another thing to keep in mind is that this is the last point in the trial where you may be given the hint to settle. As you may recall, in that case you settle.

4. Comedian Judges

You will learn more about the genus of judges later, but there is one common member of the species that you may encounter, Master of Ceremonies. Many judges tend to give vent to their frustrated vaudevillian impulses when holding Small Claims Court. To some extent, this is both refreshing and beneficial to the proceedings, since a certain amount of levity tends to dispel the more intimidating aspects of courtroom atmosphere. Indeed, when well done, some gentle ribbing from the judge can make people realize they're being a bit rigid and make them more accepting of a fair compromise decision. Even judges who aren't cracking jokes may be inclined to lay a little homely philosophical advice on you. If the judge feels you're asking too much for the dress the cleaner ruined, he may suggest a cheaper department store. He may try to put your own fender-bender into perspective with a little parable about the perils of the peripatetic society. Of course, to you, your case is no laughing matter, you came here for satisfaction, not storytelling. No matter how corny his jokes, or how condescending his observations, the best policy is to grin and bear it. He may seem to you to be running a Kangaroo Court, but it's still the bosseroo you are talking to. You may be pretty fast with a comeback yourself, and a little return humor probably isn't going to kill you. (I once saw a judge taken aback after he suggested that some of the trials and tribulations of a plaintiff were "all water under the bridge." "I know that, Your Honor," the unamused plaintiff replied, "but I still have wet feet.") Generally speaking, however, wit isn't going to help you half as much as humility.

How you react is up to you, but remember, the game is won or lost by what the judge ends up writing down on that little card he's going to fill out. And I think he's somewhat more disposed to give judgments to the "straight-man" than to a competing humorist.

Incidentally, you shouldn't view this kind of judge too harshly. Remember, he's sitting there with human nature on parade. The continued flow of righteous indignation does indeed get sort of funny after a while. There are probably times when humor is the only way of maintaining a modicum of sanity amidst all these squabbling citizens.

In summary, when you're up there flying solo, the thing to remember is that you are trying to come off as an honest yeoman with Justice and (insofar as you can manifest it) law on your side. You are trying to show you are an honest person who acted reasonably. Your strength is of the strength of ten because your heart is pure, or at least you have successfully faked it. (As you will learn in the last chapter, a little spite may come in handy too.)

Perhaps this little couplet will help you keep the essentials in mind:

> *Histrionics are to be eschewed,*
> *Organization is to be pursued.*

AFTER THE TRIAL

Whether or not the judge announces his decision immediately or "reserves" it, you will receive a postcard a few days later announcing either "judgment for the defendant," or "judgment for the plaintiff in the amount of   ." The next question that arises, depending on the outcome, is: Can the B*st*rds Appeal?

In quite a few jurisdictions, the judgment of the Small Claims Court is "conclusive" upon the plaintiff, which means the plaintiff cannot appeal. This is a sensible, nut-filtering device.

Defendants, however, may almost always appeal if they want to go through the trouble. The trouble consists of usually:

1. Filing a notice of appeal within a certain amount of time after the entry of the judgment. This is a piece of paper that for a fee paid by them will be sent to you saying that the other side is planning to appeal.

2. Filing a bond or "undertaking." This is a formal promise, backed up by their own deposit or that of a bonding company, that they will pay the judgment and costs within a certain amount of time if their appeal is denied or dismissed. This again costs money. There will also be a fee required by the appeal court.

The appeal, incidentally, depending on the jurisdiction, will be either for a whole new trial (trial de novo) or an appeal based only on the contention that there was a mistake made in applying the law. If it's an appeal on a basis of law, there will be additional expenses for transmitting records.

All of the above hassle creates a substantial disincentive to appeal from Small Claims Court judgments by either side. We should all give lusty cheers for this, since appeal certainly violates the spirit of Small Claims Court, which is to get the matter over with.

If the other side files an appeal, or a transfer that will not be remanded to SCC, it's time to go and see a lawyer. There are going to be briefs to file and other hassles to contend with. It's conceivable you might even want to do this yourself, but even so you will need the advice of a lawyer. There just seems to be no way around it.

HOW DO I COLLECT?

Well, let's suppose you've been vindicated. Now all you have to do is get paid. Suing is better than stewing, but catharsis goes best with cash. (And, as was once noted, a court "judgment" is not cash. It is more in the nature of a hunting license. The court adds up the bill, but it's up to you to collect.)

If you've sued a reasonably legitimate business, there should be no particular problem in collecting. They'll get a little post card from the court informing them that judgment has been entered against them in the sum of X dollars and directing them to pay immediately. Individuals may be a bit more slippery, but in any event, if you don't get your money in at least two weeks, you should send a letter that says something like the following:

Dear Sir:

I have been informed by the 6th District Court of Bohack that I have been awarded a judgment against you of the sum XX dollars payable immediately.

To avoid further inconvenience and expense on either of our parts, please send a check or money order to me at the above address.

Sincerely,

Now, if this letter doesn't bring your money in ten days or so, the time has come for a trip or call to the clerk's office to find out what you do next. The process of collecting from a recalcitrant debtor varies widely from state to state; but probably this is the point at which the matter will be put into the hands of the sheriff, marshal, or constable. What you are going to have to do is get a copy of a "writ of execution." This is a piece of paper which you get from the court which gives the sheriff the authority to "satisfy" the judgment out of the real or personal property of the judgment debtor.

This satisfaction is achieved by "attachment" or "garnishment." Attachment is a process in which the court takes some of the debtor's property and sells it in order to get enough money to satisfy the judgment, the debtor getting the leftover. This is the auction-on-the-courthouse-steps sort of thing. Garnishment means that the court orders the debtor's employer to pay directly to the creditor a certain amount of money each payday out of the debtor's pay until the judgment is satisfied.

Before you can get any of this rolling, however, you are going to have to get a piece of paper from the clerk which authorizes the sheriff or marshal to begin garnishment or attachment. This is called a "writ of execution" or some similar name.

Try to get it by mail and save yourself a trip to the courthouse. You'll have to enclose a check for the fee, usually a dollar or two. When the writ comes back in the mail, it's worth one last try to collect yourself without seeing the sheriff. Try the following letter:

Dear Sir:

I thought I should tell you that the court has issued a writ of execution for the judgment entered against you on (date). The writ, a copy of which is enclosed, will be passed on to the sheriff for institution of appropriate attachment or garnishment proceedings within ten days. At that point, the matter will be out of my hands.

You will, of course, have to pay the judgment, plus the costs of such attachment and garnishment proceedings, plus interest. If payment is received within ten days, however, the matter will be dropped and you will incur no further expenses.

Sincerely,

If that doesn't work it's time to call the sheriff.

As has been already mentioned, if the clerk tells you that you should go and see a sheriff or a marshal to collect, by all means go see the sheriff, not the marshal. The sheriff is a civil servant who does not get a cut of what he collects. The marshal, however, lives by fees, a percentage of the judgment collected. Therefore he will probably give your penny-ante judgment short shrift. By the way, the defendant will be liable for sheriff's or marshal's fees incurred in the course of collecting the judgment.

In a few jurisdictions, where you are not allowed to get the sheriff or marshal into the act by yourself, the process will be somewhat different. Instead of getting a "writ of execution," you get a piece of paper served on the defendant calling him to court again for an "examination of assets." This is kind of a friendly little inquiry by the judge as to exactly why the debt hasn't been paid and whether the debtor really can't afford it.

Unfortunately, whatever the jurisdiction, all of these steps are going to require time and effort on your part. If you don't want to bother, what you should do is call a lawyer and tell him you've got the judgment and that you can't collect it but that you know where the person lives and you want to know if he'd take the case. Most lawyers will be glad to take the case for about a 30 percent to 40 percent cut of the judgment, if it's anywhere over a hundred dollars. (Caution: any out-of-the-pocket expenses that may occur may have to be paid by you. This could cut down your recovery to less than 50 percent.) On the other hand, even though you get less than the full amount, the other guys have to pay the whole amount, so you still get that satisfaction. To sum up, if you have any trouble collecting, see the clerk, see the sheriff, or see a lawyer. If you don't know a lawyer, call the clerk's office and ask for the name of a "good collection lawyer."

If the other side does not have any money, not even attachment, garnishment, or the world's best collection lawyer is going to get any out of him. And even if he does have property, much of it will be statute by exempt from attachment; for example, cars that are used to go to work. Also, you can only garnish salaries above a certain amount.

If your target is "judgment proof," there is not much you can do right now. Remember, however, that your judgment is good for ten to twenty years, depending on your jurisdiction. This means that once a year you can try to attach or garnish him again, or you can haul him back into court for an examination of assets. People's financial positions change. They get jobs, they marry money, they inherit money, they win the state lottery. Furthermore, you have a right to collect interest on the judgment, plus all the costs incurred in collecting it, such as sheriff's fees. This can start adding up. (The interest is usually specified by law and ranges anywhere from 4 percent up.)

If you're really mad at the person, take advantage of your right to haul him down to court once a year for an examination of his assets. Judgment-proof welfare chiselers or not, they have to come. (See form on page 215.) Just put them on your Christmas card list and give them a little trip to court every year to start the New Year wrong. If you really feel mean, haul them in for three years, skip one, and then do it again the fifth year. After a while, if they have the money, they'll seriously begin to think about paying.

CHAPTER VI

YOUR SMALL CLAIMS COURTS CIVIL RIGHTS

Whenever you use Small Claims Court, what you are really doing is sticking up for your civil rights. Unless you have had some legal training, however, you probably have only vague notions of what these rights are. The purpose of this chapter is to expand your consciousness of them and the different situations in which you can put them to use.

The only purpose of "civil" courts, including Small Claims Courts, is to enforce the basic rights that living in a "civil"-ized society is supposed to guarantee one, like the right not to be pushed around or excessively bothered. Civil courts enforce these rights in disputes between private parties and in a special way: by requiring those who infringe on the rights of others to recompense the victim with money. This pocketbook revenge is designed both as compensation for harm suffered and as a symbolic substitute for more violent means of revenge—"taking the law into your own hands."

This point about translating the infringement of a right into money is very important, because technically, this is the only power that Small Claims Courts generally have. They do not have so-called "equity" powers, the authority to effect justice by issuing a court order to make someone do something or stop doing something. All they can do is put a price on the breach of the right being enforced.

These civil rights come from a variety of sources. Some of them have been legislated, like the civil rights we are all most familiar with—the right not to suffer racial discrimination; some of them you write yourself by entering into contracts, documents that assign rights and responsibilities to each side. And some of them stem from the "common law," that bundle of ideas on how civilized men should comport themselves inherited from Merrie Olde England.

Before going any further, however, one thing should be made perfectly clear. This "little knowledge" you acquire isn't going to make a lawyer out of you.

In case you haven't heard, the law is neither easy nor simple in its theory or application. It is a vast and nebulous web of rules and principles, counterbalancing principles and rules, amendments exceptions, and interpretations whose full scope tends to make the mind burp. The purpose of it all is to order and inject justice into all of human endeavor and it is correspondingly complex. It may help to think of it as the Great Baggie whose thin film keeps all of human society from dribbling away into an undistinguished puddle of entropy.

So those unfamiliar with the law—and that probably means you, irrespective of your education and experience—should approach Do-It-Yourself law very gingerly. The simple fact is that the way the world is set up, you need a lawyer to do most of the things that lawyers usually do. This does not mean that the world cannot and should not be re-engineered in this respect.

As matters stand, while avoiding probate may be a good idea, writing your own estate plan is not. It could lead to protracted courtroom warfare that could cost many dozens of times more than good legal advice sought at the proper time. One of the first things they tell you in law school is: "He who is his own lawyer has a fool for a client and an ass for an attorney." It is more than propaganda. The only reason representing yourself in Small Claims Court makes sense is that the system is considerably altered and modified and the amount at stake is relatively low.

Getting involved in a legal case after reading this chapter will put you roughly in the position of one stranded in the woods knowing only that moss grows thickest on the north side of the trees, following water downstream will probably lead you to civilization, and rolling yourself in a snowbank will keep you from freezing. With a little bit of luck it might get you through, providing you don't starve or trip over a grouchy bear. But neither the knowledge nor the experience will make you a woodsman.

If that's understood, we can go on to the few legal principles you will need to know.

The first is that you can't go around suing for any old thing that rumples your feathers. Your complaint must fall into some legally defined pigeonhole. You must have a legal "cause of action" which satisfies certain criteria.

These criteria are called the "elements" of your case, the basic component facts you have to "prove" in order to win. Each right you enforce involves its own set of elements. We'll talk about what "prove" means in a minute, but for the moment just remember that in theory anyway, if you fail to prove even just one element, you fail to satisfy your burden of proof.

I finally understood in law school what "elements" were all about and why it is important to think in terms of them through an example that really had to do with something else.

It turns out that in defending a case, it's perfectly all right to plead mutually exclusive propositions. This is called "pleading in the alternative." The classic example of pleading in the alternative is an old English case of the cracked teapot. This lawsuit involved a plaintiff who was suing over a teapot he lent, which was returned with a crack in it. In answer to the suit for the damage to the pot, the defendant "pleaded" the following defenses:

1. I never borrowed the pot.
2. There was no damage when I returned it.
3. It was already cracked when I borrowed it.

This example is meant to show that despite the fact that each proposition contradicts the other two, this form of pleading is perfectly correct and acceptable. The defendant can win if he can show any of the defenses, and he can try for all three.

What it also shows, however, is that the teapot owner could be foiled in his attempt at recovery if he failed to "prove" *any* of the three "elements."

1. He lent the defendant the pot.
2. The pot was sound when he lent it.
3. The pot was broken when the defendant returned it.

Indeed, there is even another element, not mentioned; the fact that the plaintiff owned the pot.

Your case, no matter what it is about, will involve a number of "elements." Many of these elements are trivial or obvious, such as the fact that the plaintiff actually owned the pot.

Therefore, in the discussion of your rights which follows, you'll often be seeing little checklists of "elements" that are the pieces of fact you need to prove to establish your cause of action.

Actually, it is more correct to say *that* you might need to prove. It will depend on the judge and his view of just how freewheeling Small Claims Court justice should be.

Take the way a Los Angeles judge disposed of a dispute over some car repairs. The case involved a mechanic (apparently the proprietor of a small gas station) who had sold a Mexican-American a car and subsequently performed needed repairs. He was now suing for the balance due on this work. Plaintiff was armed with all sorts of parts and repair orders signed by the defendant, who didn't seem to have too much to say for himself except that he couldn't afford all this money for a car. Although I was (and am) hardly intimate with California used car statutes, it seemed to me that the plaintiff had demonstrated all the "elements" of his case. This was a sale between private parties and subject to the principles of *caveat emptor* (let the buyer beware). The car having been sold "as is," the repairs having been authorized and performed, the defendant having acknowledged the debt for the repairs by making partial payments, things looked bad for the sentimental favorite —in this case, the defendant.

That's not the way the judge saw it. Peering down at the plaintiff, the judge asked what the "bluebook price" (standard used-car list value) of the car was, and received his answer. Then he asked the total amount of money that the defendant had already paid, and received an answer a couple of hundred dollars higher than the bluebook price. (Of course, there had been considerable work done on the car.) Then, fixing the mechanic with a look that George C. Patton might have reserved for a private caught trying to go over the hill, he gave him approximately the following lecture: "You mean to stand here and tell me that you've gotten $1100 out of this man for a five-year-old car and have the nerve to come here and ask for more? Well, you and your sort have another thing coming. You're not to go around cheating people and expecting this court to back you up. You're not going to get another penny out of this man as long as I'm sitting here. Judgment for the next defendant." Plaintiff's protests were cut short by a curt, "Next case."

We have seen that a judge has vast discretion in Small Claims Court; but the list of the rules of jurisprudence that were shot to smithereens by doing what the judge did in the way that he did it is a very long one. I'll spare you the details, but there is just no way that what that judge did was "legal" in Small Claims or any other court.

After the session, in the course of our conversation, I brought up the case and the legal issues involved, intending to examine gently the jurisprudential philosophy underlying such an extraordinary *modus operendi*. Once more, the judge cut to the heart of the matter. "Look, we both know what happened. This guy saw a defenseless sucker coming, sold him a piece of junk, and charged him through the nose to fix it up. He got plenty of money out of that car, and I'll be damned if I'm going to make the buyer pay him more." He didn't exactly add "Case dismissed," but I got the point. Here was a man who felt that ignoring the letter of the law was perfectly just in order to fulfill its basic purpose and wasn't afraid to take a reasonable guess about what happened (about which he was almost certainly correct).

Contrast this attitude with the New York judge who was confronted with a long, complicated case involving an employment broker suing for a fee.

The judge was presented with two conflicting stories. He could either believe one over the other, or not make any "factual" judgment as to which story was the truth. If he refrained from making the judgment, the legal decision-making standards dictated that the plaintiff had not sufficiently "proved" his case against the defendant.

Again, I'll spare you the details, but it seemed to me the defendant was a liar and the plaintiff was entitled to his fee. But there was no evidence except the plaintiff's "self-serving" testimony. So, the judge found for the defendant.

The case happened to be the last of the evening. A few minutes later I interviewed the judge in his chamber. As we were just beginning to talk, I mentioned that I had found the case interesting and felt that the very fact the plaintiff had bothered to bring the case argued on his side. "You know," he said, shaking his head and pursing his lips in disgust, "I just knew that bastard (the defendant) was lying. But there was nothing I could do about it. There was just not enough evidence." Here was an honest judge obviously upset by what he had "had to do," but scrupulously adhering to the standard of regular court.

The first kind of judge, the one ready to sweep away the legalisms and get "to the heart" of the matter, I call a *fundamentalist*. The second kind, who is more reticent to take advantage of all the powers his Small Claims Court role affords him and sticks more rigidly to formal legal decision-making rules, I call a *formalist*.

Most judges actually fall between the above extremes, but the lesson is to prepare your case for a formalist and hope you get a fundamentalist.

You should be in theory, then, prepared to "prove" all the elements of your case. How are you supposed to do this?

In practical terms, the answer is the best way that you can. There really are four kinds of proof that come into play in the Small Claims Court situation:

1. Physical Evidence, including documents—receipts, contracts, the damaged goods, photographs, etc.

2. Testimony—by neutral witnesses.

3. Testimony—biased witnesses, your friends, relatives, or someone with a stake in the outcome.

4. Your own unsupported testimony.

The first kind of proof is better than the second kind, and so forth. However, lots of times you will only have the fourth kind. That's all right, as long as you didn't overlook any opportunity to use better evidence. If you lost the sales slip and can't prove the dress the cleaner ruined cost $245 four months ago, okay, but before you go in there with just your word, call the store and see if you can get their copy of the slip or other verification of cost. If it happens to be a store you are suing and you need the slip, use your subpoena power. If the thing you are complaining about is a dishwasher, you obviously can't bring it in, but if it's a toaster, why not? It's a symbol of your outrage even if you can't plug it in.

There's no mystery in the idea of proving a fact in the best way you are able to. And if you can't, don't give up the ship; for all you know the judge won't even be bothered; but it just looks better all around and in some situations may be very important.

To summarize:

You have lots of "civil" rights under the law. The way these rights are enforced is by a court order ordering those who break them to pay you money for the damage you have suffered. In order to collect, you must be able to show that the situation you are complaining about has all the "elements" necessary to the enforcement of that right, or at least convince a fundamentalist judge that right is on your side.

Turning to specifics on exactly what civil rights you have, a good place to start is with some of the most basic ones of all, your "tort" rights.

A tort is neither a small pastry nor an Elizabethan bawd. It is a breach of a duty owed to you as a member of society. Tort rights are reflections of the terms of the Social Contract, the basic rules and regulations which govern the way we act toward each other. Tort rights are rooted in English "Common Law." As you will see, the common law is in turn rooted in common sense.

Your tort rights are best phrased as rights *not* to have something happen to you. Here are a few of the most important ones, along with examples of situations in which you might want to exercise them in Small Claims Court:

You have a right not to be manhandled, pushed around, or intimidated by force (Assault and Battery).

This is about the most fundamental right I can conceive of, the right to the integrity of your own body. Let's say some repressed flasher in the office keeps playing pinchy-pinchy with your bum-bum. And he won't take the hint to confine his hands to his own crotch, as is his custom. Well, if you've given him fair warning, and you've got a witness . . . you've got a lawsuit.

Or you were peacefully riding your ten-speed bike, trying to figure out what on earth you were going to use fourth, seventh, and ninth for, when a carload of young citizens zooms by, yelling, jeering, and screaming, playing a modern version of what seems to be "get a horse." You pull up at the light and there they are again. This time some little hood flips a cigarette at you as they go by. Well, if you can get the license number (and thus track him down), you've got a lawsuit.

In both cases above, or in any other number of all-too-normal situations in the world we live in, you have been assaulted and/or battered. Assault and battery are generally thought of as a crime, which they are. However, acts can be simultaneously criminal and civil wrongs. He or she by whom you are assaulted can be taken to jail and be sued civilly.

In serious cases, the "damages" resulting from these two torts (you'll see the difference in a moment) as in any personal injury, exceed the Small Claims limit. But in less serious, but still galling and sometimes potentially dangerous instances, although the legal damages aren't spectacular, the annoyance is substantial enough to want to teach the offender a lesson. If this is the case in some occurrence you are involved in, here are the elements you need to sue. Strictly speaking, although both torts are usually found together, there is a distinction between assault and battery. Both require:

1. *An act by the defendant*: words by themselves are not enough for either assault or battery. If the town bully says, "I'm going to pulverize you, creep," no battery, and, as we shall see, no assault unless you believe him. To prove that you believed him, you probably have to show in some concrete fashion that you actually *did* believe him—for example, fleeing or even taking a step backward or perhaps just raising your hand as a gesture of self-defense.

2. *Intent*: the perpetrator must actually intend to assault or batter. In searching for intent the court asks whether the defendant must have been substantially certain that an assault or battery would result. For example, if he throws the rest of his malted milk out of the window and it lands on you, he has probably battered you. (And if he hasn't, he's been negligent anyway.) Or, if he is rushing headlong in a crowd because he is late and knocks you down, he has battered you. In both of these examples, he should have known that a harmful or offensive physical contact would result from his conscious act. Therefore, he would be liable because he had legal "intent."

3. *Causation*: the assault or battery must *legally*

be *caused* by the defendant's act or by some
force set in motion by it. This legal causation
requirement is satisfied if the defendant's conduct is a "substantial factor" in bringing about
the harm. Basically, the only time this test is
not successfully met is if some *deus ex machina*
intervenes during the course of the episode in
question. Boss chases secretary around desk
with intention of kissing her. At that moment
(and not because of the vibrations), a ceiling
fixture falls off and injures her. No battery, but
(as we shall see) assault.

Act, intent, causation. These are the elements common to two torts. There is one more: "harmful or
offensive contact." The difference between assault and
battery is that battery requires actual physical contact
by the perpetrator or some force he has put in motion
(the rock he threw), while an assault is mainly in the
mind of the victim. It requires only fear that you are
going to be touched in a way that may harm, offend or
disgust you. (Note that you don't have to be frightened,
just disgusted.) And it is sufficient that the perpetrator
have the *apparent* ability, even if not the *actual* ability,
to perform the assault—e.g., a eunuch threatening rape,
or more to the point, a person holding an unloaded or
even toy gun (so long as you don't *know* the gun can't
really hurt you).

Of course, no right is absolute. There are "defenses,"
legal excuses, for acts that the law would otherwise
consider torts. For assault and battery, probably the
most important are self-defense and consent.

Consent can be found both in actual permission
(Kiss me, you fool!) or the circumstances surrounding
the incident—being merely jostled in a crowd that you
chose to be in.

Thus, in line with these examples of male-female
assaults, there does come a point in these matters where
silence is considered consent. If a man is making it
pretty clear that he has designs on temporarily suspend-
ing your virtue and you have not bothered to contradict

the blueprint, then you should remember that the law takes into account the surrounding circumstances. As one judge once put it, "There's no harm in asking." And with these types of invitations, consent is:

Not so much an invitation
As lack of manifested disinclination.

Another personal right you have is the right not to be "falsely imprisoned." False imprisonment in this sense does not mean being wrongly put in jail, but being held someplace against your will. The elements of this tort are act, intent, causation—as in assault and battery, and confinement, meaning a detention of the plaintiff within some boundaries for a time, however short, against the plaintiff's will. One common example of false imprisonment would be your detention in a store by an over-zealous management that wrongfully suspected you of shoplifting, although reasonable cause or (in some jurisdictions) statutory authorization might be a defense. Generally, however, anyone who keeps you someplace against your will better have a pretty good reason.

In addition to the personal tort civil rights, you also have property tort civil rights, under which you can sue civilly for such things as unauthorized invasion of your land ("trespass"). Except for the tort of "conversion," which allows you to sue someone for the value of what he stole from you, it is doubtful that you would have much occasion to use any of them.

I have never seen a Small Claims Court suit for an intentional tort, although I have a friend who sued an airline for false imprisonment over a dispute revolving around payment for switching his ticket from coach to first class in mid-flight. (It's a long story involving an argument between him and a stewardess. On landing, he was surrounded by airline personnel who "escorted" him to the ticket counter without touching him, but causing him to be virtually imprisoned within this circle. He lost a technically good case apparently because of Perry Masonitis.)

Nevertheless, if the occasion arises, that's what the courts—and the torts—are there for.

All of the torts we have so far discussed have been "intentional," that is they require that the defendant more or less intend to know with "substantial certainty" that he would cause such a result. In return for the heavier burden of proving this intent, the law gives the plaintiff a sort of backside break regarding damages. Unlike all other sorts of civil cases, where you must prove you suffered damages as a result of the tort, when it comes to an intentional tort you get *something*, even if you suffered no apparent damage. What that something totals up to is totally within the discretion of the court. Thus, in the example of the kids almost causing you to fall off your bike, what you would probably do (assuming no actual injuries) is sue for a nice round number, say $200, and let the court decide how expensive the lesson should be. If what you sue for is a reasonable slap on the wrist, you should stand a good chance of getting it.

NEGLIGENCE IN A NUTSHELL

You have a right to be compensated for injuries received due to the carelessness of others. As part of the social contract, we all have a duty to one another or "due care," that is, a duty to act as a "reasonable person" would under the circumstances of whatever we happen to be doing. If you are careless and through your carelessness someone is harmed, you are going to have to foot the bill.

This, in oversimplified brief, is what the tort of negligence is all about. If you've been harmed by someone's carelessness, here are the elements you have to show to collect.

1. A Duty of Due Care. This duty is measured by the "reasonable person" test, which couldn't be simpler: "How would the average reasonable person of plaintiff's age, intelligence, and experience, have conducted himself under the same circumstances?" The reasonable person is really something of a paragon and must be a very boring acquaintance since he is so careful in all situations. The specific duties of due care we all have are, it turns out, as innumerable as the stars above and as varied as every conceivable set of circumstances.

2. *Breach of the Duty.* This breach can come about by an act (driving too fast to be able to stop to avoid hitting the car in front of you) or a failure to act (neglecting to repair the rickety stairway the visitor fell through).

3. *Cause.* The limits and extent of "causation" are the great battleground of torts. You have to start showing off that "except for the defendant's negligent act you would not have been harmed." But this alone is not sufficient connection. You will probably have to show that the result you are complaining of was a reasonable proximate; a reasonably foreseeable result. Any further analysis leads us into a quagmire of metaphysical rationalizations. Negligence is simply one of those areas where each case is different. If you feel you have been harmed through someone's carelessness, just file suit and tell your story to the judge. Chances are your instincts will be correct.

Incidentally, in a suit for negligence, the court looks at the way a plaintiff acted, also. If the damages are partly a result of your own negligence (he went through the light and hit you, but it was 10 P.M. and you were driving with your lights off), you may be "contributorily negligent" and will be ineligible to collect.

What follows are a few examples of some negligence-related rights you might want to exercise in Small Claims Court, and some of the wrinkles you may encounter in doing so. Otherwise, if you would like to know more about the sorts of things people sue for, go to a legal library and ask for "Prosser on Torts," which should satisfy your curiosity, or at least drown it.

You have a right not to have your baggage lost or damaged.

Occasionally an airliner, train, bus, or other "common carrier" will lose or damage your baggage. When that happens, you go through the company's internal complaint procedure, which involves filling out forms and dealing with a complaint adjuster.

The job of the complaint adjuster is to adjust the complaint at least cost to his employer. On the other hand, I have gone through this procedure a couple of times with airlines, and they have always been honest, cheerful, and ready to make what I thought was a fair and agreeable adjustment. I have, however, heard of a number of cases involving other "carriers" (such as bus companies) that did not turn out as happily.

The first important thing to remember is not to allow yourself to be persuaded to fill out a form that contains less than the full amount lost. If you need more space to list what was in the suitcase, ask for another form. If they've lost one of two suitcases, and you're not sure what you put in the lost one, don't sign anything until you go home and unpack the other one. If you're not sure of the valuation of any items, make out the form to the best of your ability right there, but ask if you can take it home, finish it, and mail it in.

Sometimes, if the damage is minor, such as scratched or dented luggage, the claim will be settled right there, and you will get your check by mail. For larger claims, say over $50, the adjuster may make you an offer, or may just file the claim. Basically, "common carriers" don't like to be taken into court any more than you like to go through the trouble of doing so; so reasonable arrangements can usually be worked out. You should keep in mind that you're not going to be compensated either by the carrier or by the Small Claims Court, if it comes to that, for the replacement value of your goods. Rather, you will get the fair market value.

The fun usually begins if you lost a suitcase and there is some sort of fine print limitation on the back of the ticket that essentially says "we are liable only up to a certain amount of money. If you want more insurance, you have to buy it." The claims people are going to point to this, and refuse to offer you anything over the limit, which is often only $50.

This is a case you would take to Small Claims Court.

The law involved is basically that the carrier has a right to set a reasonable limit to the amount of money it will pay for lost or damaged goods. However, you, on the other hand, have a right to fair notice of this policy. Fine point on the back of a baggage stub may simply not be fair notice.

This is the kind of case where it comes in handy to have a sympathetic judge. Basically, all you can do is go in and say, "Well, there were no signs around, the fine print was too small for me to read without my glasses (which were in my suitcase)," or "I wouldn't mind if they'd tell you, I'd be glad to pay the extra money, but sneaking it in on the back of the ticket where it's almost invisible is unfair."

Furniture movers, by the way, are not common carriers, but private carriers; however, they are liable for damage or loss that results from their negligence. If you pack a teapot with reasonable care and it wasn't cracked when you packed it, you can probably get yourself another teapot. Once again, count on dealing with some sort of settlement procedure, which will try to drive the best bargain it can.

You have a "Right" not to be injured by products "negligently" designed or manufactured.

The law books are filled with incidences in which a product not only fails to perform as advertised, but also causes burns, lacerations, sickness, or any number of the other innumerable possible forms of injury to the user. Most "product liability" cases, as they are called, involve damages far above the level for Small Claims Court, and are handled by specialized lawyers on a contingency fee basis.

On the other hand, not all injuries are major. If Junior hurts himself on a dangerous toy badly enough for a trip to the hospital for a stitch or two, but the lawyer you consulted says that going to court isn't worth the trouble, by all means sue the store, and/or the toy distributor, and/or the manufacturer, depending on whom you can serve. Claim the medical expenses, the mileage on the car for the trip to the hospital, and any time you lost from work taking the child to the hospital.

You should also add on a reasonable amount for the child's pain and suffering, an amount equal to all the other expenses you suffered, or even the amount that brings you up to the limit, but be prepared not to collect it. After all, injuring yourself on toys, defective or not, is part of growing up. As the old saying goes, "You eat a peck of dirt and bleed a barrel of blood before you die." Whatever the rationalization, judges are very loath to give small claims damages for pain and suffering. But, in this case, there's no harm in asking for a reasonable amount, and if the judge is sympathetic you might get it.

There is, incidentally, one important non-financial benefit from these kinds of suits. Win or lose in financial terms, you stand a pretty good chance of getting that menace off the counter of that particular store anyway. If that's all that such a suit accomplishes, it could save some child having his eye poked out.

This may be all you really want to accomplish; in that case, just tell the store in negotiations that you will be satisfied if they reimburse you for actual expenses and agree to get rid of the toy. Otherwise, you should pursue the case. If they are sane, they will breathe a sigh of relief and be glad to do so.

The elements of a products liability case are:

1. That you bought the item from the defendant or the defendant manufactured the item. If you received it as a gift, sue anyway, but you might have some trouble.

2. That there was a "defect" in the item. The defect can be in negligent design (a "tippy" chair), negligent manufacture (darts with tips that children can easily pull off), or simply failure to warn of a hidden danger (color that will wipe off on your clothes, or clothing that is highly flammable).

3. That the item was being put to normal or reasonably foreseeable use. (It's probably reasonably foreseeable that a chair will be used as a stool occasionally.)

4. Causal connection between the defect claimed and the injury caused.

You have a right to get your clothes back from the cleaners in no worse shape than you left them.

The only solution to having dry cleaners ruin occasional garments is to use the coin-operated machines and ruin an occasional garment yourself. These things happen. Your favorite woolen coat comes back feeling like it was dumped in glue, and there's nothing anyone on this earth can do to reincarnate its former classy soft woven splendor. Nor is the compensation you are legally entitled to sufficient to reimburse you for the pain, suffering, and inconvenience of the loss. *C'est la vie.*

Dry cleaners are accustomed to handling complaints. They are also quite aware that they are responsible only to the extent of the fair market value of the goods. Their settlement offer is going to reflect this. Your attitude toward it, in turn, should reflect the fact that no one ever loses a suit against dry cleaners in Small Claims Court. But, the defendant always manages to get something hacked off the original price, usually one-third, and somewhat more if the garment is older.

One thing you do not have to reconcile yourself to, however, is being bound by any signs or fine print purporting to limit the dry cleaner's liability to 10 dollars or whatever. Simply tell the dry cleaner that you don't believe they enforce these clauses in court. You might give him a hint by adding, "Particularly in Small Claims Court." Incidentally, why should you be doing business with a dry cleaner who has that sort of sign up in the first place?

Finally, if you have basic trust in the dry cleaner you have been dealing with, you may find him more willing to settle if you are in turn willing to take it out in trade.

CONTRACTS IN A CAPSULE: YOU HAVE A RIGHT NOT TO BE GYPPED.

A contract is an agreement, a deal, an exchange of promises to do or not to do something. A contract may be oral or written, expressed or implied. (A good example of an implied contract is a roommate's duty to pay for his long-distance calls even though the phone is in your name.) Contracts are part of everyday life. Every time you buy an item, from a pallazzo to a ham sandwich, you and the seller have executed a contract.

Contract law is once again one of those areas far too complicated to consider on any but the most superficial level. Just remember this: if you did what you promised when you said you would do it (e.g., paid for something), you are entitled to what you paid for (that something is the condition that was promised).

Small Claims Courts contract suits involve mainly shoddy goods or shoddy services. When they involve goods, the suit revolves around a breach of the warranty, either express or implied. An express warranty is the "guarantee" you get from the manufacturer. An implied warranty, which you get thanks to the Uniform Commercial Code, in effect in all states except Louisiana, says that you are entitled to get goods that are reasonably fit for the purpose for which they were sold, i.e. they must work right. If they do not, sue the store.

In cases of disputes over shoddy workmanship, as discussed in "How Much To Sue For?" you should count on paying the workman something, unless he completely botched the job. When dealing with workmen, incidently, you will save yourself a lot of trouble if you will do two things:

1. Check with the Better Business Bureau (listed in the phone book), which keeps files on complaints received about businessmen and rates them A, B, C, or D. Never accept less than a B, and go for an A if one is available.

2. Sit down and try to specify everything from the time schedule to exact grade of materials. You'll understand each other better for the experience and head off a lot of disputes and disappointments.

It has seemed more sensible to organize most of what you should know about contracts around the specific examples as they will and have come up in the book, such as the rule about interpreting any ambiguities in contracts against the drafter.

The one other main face of contract law you should know a little about is fraud.

How do you know when you have been defrauded? Basically, if you have been conned, duped, gulled, enticed, bamboozled, or otherwise persuaded to part with your money because of a lie or "misrepresentation," you have been defrauded.

Jaundiced institutions that they are, courts tend to take the skeptical view of a dissatisfied customer's memory of what went on at the sale. Like the con who cries, "I was framed," the buyer who cries, "I was tricked" may find his words fail to inspire instant belief.

Thus, fraud falls into the category of what the law terms "disfavored defenses," which means that the party asserting fraud has a heavy "burden" of proof to maintain. (It's called a defense because fraud is used as a defense for the obligations incurred in making a bargain, or to "undo" the bargain completely.) Even if you have really been defrauded, you are faced with something of an uphill fight and may not be able to prove it satisfactorily to the judge. A lot will depend upon your presentation.

More specifically, the law divides the offense into five elements:

1. An act or statement ("misrepresentation"),
2. that the defendant knew or should have known was false ("scienter"),
3. used to bait the hook ("intention"),
4. that snagged the fish ("reliance" on the statement),
5. who is now trying to get off the hook ("damages").

So, fraud is sort of a breach of promise that the maker knew was false to begin with. There is a level at which that accusation constitutes fightin' words, which is another reason for the disfavored defense status of fraud.

Your capacity to be defrauded is a function of your degree of innocence, credulousness, or tendency to trust people and of your sophistication. The law recognizes a general idea of excessively higher sucker-quotient, and tied up with the disfavored defense notion is the idea that there are some limits to innocence. That is, there is a point at which the law says simply "If you're that stupid, you deserve everything you get." This limit is expressed in the legal concept of a certain amount of tolerable "puffery" on the part of salesmen who sell you the Maserati or outboard motor "owned by a little old lady and only driven on Sundays." As one of my favorite law professors once put it: "If you can't cheat a fool, what else are they for?" The law does not help fools, and neither does Small Claims Court.

A man who had spent a couple of hundred dollars on a local radio advertising campaign for his mail-order cosmetics didn't get too far in Small Claims Court when he sued for his money back saying the radio station had promised to increase his sales and hadn't. The judge just told the plaintiff that even if the salesman had said that (which the salesman of course denied), he should have had enough sense as a businessman to figure out that no one could make that sort of guarantee.

What all this adds up to for you in Small Claims Court can be summed up in the little maxim: "Argue fraud, don't plead it." That is, zing the idea in under the judge's radar.

Hence, since being defrauded is based on a spontaneous state of mind, your presentation should try to recapture that spontaneity rather than appearing calculated or contrived. In line with the general rule of sticking to simple language, the idea is not to mention the word fraud, but to make that concept pop into the judge's mind through your use of the mother tongue. Mentioning any legal terms (God forbid you should utter the word "scienter") simply arouses too much suspicion that you are fitting the facts to the idea of fraud rather than vice versa.

If you're trying to make out a case for fraud, then the crucial point in your presentation is the description of how and why you reached the decision. You have to establish that you were *induced by* the misrepresentation ("suckered"), that there is a *causality* between the misrepresentation and your decision to buy or sign or whatever. You have to prove you were a reasonable sucker.

Thus, you should be describing the conversation between you and the salesman and his promises. "He said the machine was the best buy in the store because it would remove all particles from pots and pans," or "he told me I was sure to be able to pick up Channel 99." Then, you should establish the causality, but in ordinary words. "And so, based on that, I bought it. . . ." "That's what decided me right there. . . ." "I was kind of wavering, so I said, ' Are you sure?' and he answered, 'Absolutely.' . . . That was the aspect that I was most interested in."

By the way, your case will be considerably aided if you have laid the groundwork as suggested in Chapter Two on effective complaining, since all of your assertions will at least be on paper, and the other side may have failed to deny them when they had the chance.

So, if you bought something, and the salesman promised you something a reasonable person might believe, and it turned out not to be the case, you should give fraud a try.

If you manage to persuade the judge that there's a legitimate fraud, he will usually do something that he is technically not allowed to do, namely "undo" the transaction. In other words, he'll tell you to give the thing back and get your money. (This is called "rescission," and is interference with a transaction, something strictly speaking only within the power of a court of "equity," which Small Claims Courts usually are not.)

Or, if you want to keep whatever it is that you purchased but you want to have it repaired—or have had it repaired—so as to bring it up to the standard of that you were led to believe it was when you bought it, you can technically do that. If you really need the thing, and he cannot or will not fix it, and you can have it repaired for less than the purchase price, you can take a chance on having someone else repair it and then sue for that amount of money. (Say, for example, you came to the city to buy something to take back to the country—like a snowmobile. They knew you needed it and suckered you into buying it. You can have it repaired for less where you are than going to the expense of bringing it back to the place of purchase.) Or, you can get an estimate and bring that into court, if time is not as pressing and you want to play it safer. Once again, always keep in mind that you are going to have to convince the judge that you have acted reasonably.

As a strategic matter, however, you probably have a better chance of just undoing the sale, since you seem less to be wanting to have your cake and eat it too. In that case the judge is going to be much more inclined to treat it as an "as is" sale.

What I would do is to sue for the full value of the item, then after you've told your story to the judge explain that you are willing to keep the item if the other side will pay to have it repaired, which would cost such and such amount of money. If the judge is sympathetic to your side of the case, he will probably give the other side the choice of getting back the merchandise and returning your money or of paying you the cost of repairs or, perhaps, of repairing it himself.

By the way, when buying anything secondhand, even in a private sale, if the seller makes any warranties or representations, draw up a little "bill of sale" and write down the essentials. "Outboard motor, good running condition." If the motor has an overheating problem or something, you are in much better condition to plead fraud or breach of contract.

The fraud-type argument may come in handy against insurance companies that refuse to pay a claim because they claim the accident or whatever isn't covered by the policy. If you thought it was because of assurances by the salesman and can convincingly show this (say your spouse understood the same thing), the judge may well decide you have been defrauded. Your chances for collecting are reasonably decent especially if the document is in ridiculously fine print or absurd legaleze, which they usually are.

Also, remember that "ambiguous" terms in contracts are supposed to be interpreted "against" the party who wrote the contract, on the same general principle that the kid who splits the candy bar gets the smaller piece. All you have to do is have a plausible interpretation favorable to you of any term in the contract and make the judge believe it is so to defeat the other side under this doctrine, which the judge of course may or may not subscribe to or recall, and the contract will be interpreted that way. Arguing this point, you would say something like: "Your Honor, it's hard for me to know what this contract means since I didn't write it and it's quite technical, but it seems to me this term says . . ."

Fraud is an extremely powerful civil right if argued correctly. Always ask yourself if you have been defrauded.

CHAPTER VII

YOUR TENANT
SCC CIVIL RIGHTS

Small Claims Courts are a proper forum for exercising only some of the civil rights you have as a tenant. What SCC's do not decide is possession, that nine-tenths of the law around which most landlord-tenant disputes revolve. Disputes over repairs are also normally outside the province of the court. What Small Claims Courts do hear are the money gripes arising out of the L-T relationship—the unreturned security deposit, the catsup-stained wallpaper, the six-months past-due rent. But the matter of continued ensconcement versus out-in-the-street for you, your lover, or your Great Dane, is heard in another branch of the lower state court system in an eviction proceeding that may be known by a variety of names like summary process, forcible entry, or dispossessory hearing. As it turns out, the most frequent SCC situations seem to involve: (1) security deposits; (2) broken leases; (3) deposits to hold; and combinations of all three. Before jumping into specifics, however, threading through a few of the themes underlying the law's view of the landlord-tenant relationship will be effort well spent.

Unlike other areas of the law, which rest on common-sense notions of fairness, the law of landlord and tenant embodies some strange concepts because of its origins in the feudal relationships among lord, knight, and vassal.

The traditional "common law" view of the matter is short and (for the landlord) sweet. The tenant promises to pay rent to the landlord and to refrain from "waste," or damages to the premises. In return, the landlord promises to leave the tenant alone and not much more, that is, to provide "quiet enjoyment" of the premises. The common law view, which is still quite influential in most jurisdictions, embodies no concept of the landlord as a guarantor of services or the quality of living conditions. In the bad old days the tenant took the premises "as is." Conditions, except for hidden defects, could not later be used as an excuse for breaking a lease or reducing the rent. The landlord was not even responsible for injuries to a tenant or his guest resulting from the rotten floorboard or broken bannister. In addition, the landlord's and tenant's promises to each other were considered "independent," that is, no heat did not mean no rent. In the pure tradition, not even destruction of the premises was enough to relieve the tenant of the responsibility of paying rent to the end of the lease term.

These days, as a result of less backward-looking judicial decisions and various statutory revisions, the law in some jurisdictions is moving toward looking at the rental of property more like a contract for services than the carving of a feudal estate. Housing and sanitary codes often set a minimum level of required maintenance; statutes specify forms, time requirements, and permitted reasons for notice to vacate; and some statutes even provide for legal rent withholding for dwellings not up to code, or that contracts for such apartments are void and unenforceable. (Rent strikes and other new strategies are beyond the scope of this book and require expert advice from a lawyer or tenant group.) A few jurisdictions even depart from common law principles so far as to recognize a basic warranty of "habitability" or "fitness for human occupancy," that is, an implied promise from the landlord that the premises are fit to live in and will remain so—this latter guarantee necessarily implying a duty to maintain the property. Under this doctrine, tenants may argue that breach of this warranty relaxes or eliminates the duty to pay rent.

A related idea is that of "constructive eviction," that is, being virtually driven out of the premises by some condition that makes it impossible to live in, for example, no heat or bad leaks. In borderline cases, less drastic conditions might suffice. A Manhattan July without air conditioning might so deprive one of enjoyment of the premises as to justify premature termination of the lease. (Please do not get any bright ideas along this line without consulting a lawyer, however, or you might find yourself liable for two rents.)

Although landlord-tenant is a rapidly changing area of the law and these modern notions may have infiltrated your jurisdiction, there are still many residual situations in which the law "falls back" on common law principles; and traditional landlord-tenant principles are still quite important in the thinking of most lower court judges irrespective of the law. These men were inculcated with these ideas at law school decades ago and have lived with them all their lives. In addition, they belong to the social class more likely to own than rent. Indeed, it is quite possible that the judge will be less than abreast of some of the fancy new theories that may now be the law in his jurisdiction.

The lesson here is not to be afraid to use the old theories if they fit into the favorable side of your case. If your summer sublet was driven out by a plague of roaches in mid-July, giving legally insufficient (although loud and clear) notice and paying no rent, you should sue for all three months at the end of August. Your argument would be that the agreement was for three months, that you never promised him a rose garden or much of anything else for that matter ("I thought it was understood that he took it as is, Your Honor."); and that he is thus bound to pay rent under his side of the bargain. If you're the sublessee, on the other hand, you argue that the hoard of insects made the place literally unfit to live in (constructive eviction). If your case comes out unsatisfactorily under traditional principles, perhaps some of the arguments in the examples that follow will help. In any event you should call a local tenant or consumer protection group and see if there is any legislation on the subject. If so, and it helps you, you would be prudent to take a xerox along for the judge.

Turning to specifics, by far the most numerous class of landlord-tenant disputes revolve around security deposits. Strategy and tactics for each of the standard situations follow.

Getting Your Security Deposit Back When You Leave at the End of the Lease.

Funny thing about some landlords. If you're a week late with the rent, you'll get a notice or a phone call outlining his precise obligations to the bank and leaving no doubt whatsoever on how to assure your rent reaches him. But when it comes time to collect that extra month's rent you gave him to cover possible damage to the apartment or rent owing on departure, he becomes more elusive than Howard Hughes. And when you finally track him down, he says that the deposit will barely cover the cleaning fee, or some similar nonsensical fantasy.

In fact, what started out as a sensible idea has in many areas of the country (particularly those with a large and transient student population) become an excuse for institutionalized robbery. The condition has been so outrageous that reluctant legislatures have passed security deposit laws dictating that they be held in special accounts, that interest be paid on them, and providing triple damages against landlords who wrongfully withhold them. Some landlords still remain undeterred.

Publicity over this practice and a dawning realization of how limited the landlord's leverage at the end of the leasing period is (exactly what can he do to you if you are leaving in a few weeks anyway?) are leading more and more people to solve this problem of collecting their security deposit in the simplest way possible—withholding the last month's rent and putting the burden of extracting money on the landlord. This, of course, is technically a breach of contract. So it stands as one of life's little ironies that the most scrupulously honest people, who dutifully pay their last month's rent on time, are the ones who end up getting cheated.

Okay, you played by the rules. But the brownie points you are going to get in heaven are not cash in hand. The landlord talks about scratches and scuffs on the floor and that cigarette burn in the couch the drunk left on the night of that boffo party that established you as a living legend in your own time. On the other hand, the couch was beginning to age during Roosevelt's first administration, and although you are willing to take a few bucks off, the landlord sniffs that it is going to take him "at least" the full amount of your security deposit to replace the priceless artifact.

The route from there, of course, leads straight to Small Claims Court. The key words to remember in this situation are "normal wear and tear" because that is what you are not liable for. The fact that the carpeting is a little worn in spots, the wallpaper a microshade dirtier, the refrigerator wheezing somewhat more asthmatically, etc., is not the kind of damage for which the landlord may deduct.

This is where pictures and witnesses who saw the apartment at the beginning and at the end come in handy. I've sometimes heard the idea of taking "before" pictures, but this seems over-paranoid and underpractical, unless there is obvious damage when you move in for which you might be blamed. Just as good is an inspection listing conditions—cigarette burns, chipped enamel, which the landlord might not have noticed—and appending it to the lease. If you don't have this, and there is damage you caused, a picture of it might come in handy if the landlord verbally expands the proportions of it.

Furthermore, the landlord is bound by the same legal rules of damages you are. He must prove his damages and he may collect only the value of the damaged item or reasonable repair cost. You burn a hole in a ten-year-old rug, he gets the cost of the rug minus ten years depreciation; in theory, this might even bring it down to less than zero, but you should count on losing a few bucks. If there really is some damage that you feel is being inflated, get your own estimate, taking into account that you should in good conscience pay the workman for his time if you have no intention of using him.

Getting Your Security Deposit Back if You Leave Before the End of Your Lease.

Rich men often grumble in private that their lives are run by their tax accountants. Well, we all have our crosses to bear, and for tenants the constraint on freedom and mobility often takes form of a lease. The problem of leaving your present domain for greener, or perhaps just cheaper, sunnier, larger, or safer urban pastures can be complicated by a couple of factors if you have a lease.

In traditional jurisdictions, and there are still plenty around, if you break the lease and depart, the landlord may be under no obligation to rent the apartment and can theoretically wait until the end of the lease and sue you for the entire rent due.

The landlord who is holding your security deposit, generally isn't inclined to give it up, and may be backed up by a seemingly ironclad lease provision. For example, in many leases there is a paragraph that says something like if you wish to vacate the apartment after residing there for six or more months, you may, but must pay the landlord a sum equal to one month's rent. This is supposed to compensate him for the time and trouble it takes to rent the apartment again. The way things work in the apartment-short urban areas where you find these leases, the landlord can rent the apartment at a higher rent for a five dollar ad and a couple of hours work. If this turns out to be the situation, you can probably use Small Claims Court to get between half to all of that security deposit back.

Maximizing your chances of doing this involves going about things in the right way. You should notify your landlord (by certified mail, return receipt requested) of your intention to leave. The lease will specify the period of notice required. In that same letter, you should offer to find someone to take over the rest of the lease for you. Thus your letter will be simultaneously a notice of intention to vacate and an application to sublease.

If the landlord says that's okay with him, fine. (But be careful about whom you give the apartment to; the ultimate responsibility for damage and rent remains on you until the end of the leasehold. If the subtenants skip or demolish the place, the landlord may sue you and collect. Your only recourse then is against the subtenants.) As a sublessee, incidentally, you generally "step into the shoes" of the lessee, holding the same rights in relation to the landlord as your predecessor.

Usually, however, the landlord will prefer to choose his own tenants. In particular, he will almost surely not allow you to sublease if he plans to raise the rent. (If he is in a rent-controlled jurisdiction, allowing a subtenant effectively prevents him from getting a rent rise; if he is not rent-controlled but is an experienced landlord, he will realize that the subtenant consciously or subconsciously will resent the rent rise if he knows the previous rent, and take every opportunity to be a complaining tenant. Armchair psychology, but quite accurate.)

At any rate, after this move, you are in a pretty strong Small Claims Court position: You look as though you have been honest and reasonable, always half the battle; you can argue that you have been unreasonably refused permission to sublet. It will always state in your lease that you must apply to the landlord for permission to sublet; sometimes, however, it is added that "such permission will not be unreasonably withheld." Even without this being explicitly stated, this may in fact be the legal rule in your jurisdiction. And if you had been allowed to sublet reasonably, the landlord would have suffered no damages. (Actually, it is a very nice legal question whether you were applying for permission to sublet within the strict meaning of that term, since you were not planning to return. However, most landlords, and the majority of judges and lawyers, won't be quick enough to point that out when you spring the argument on them. In any event, they are the "drafters" of the agreement (even if it is a form), and as we have seen, the legal rule is that any ambiguities in agreements are to be construed against the drafter of the agreement.)

Unreasonable refusal of permission to sublet is the first argument to put forward because only under this one will you get your full deposit back. (Also, putting forward a plausible argument on why you should get all of the money back will be a psychological boost to your back-up position of getting some of it back.)

You should phrase yourself informally as always, perhaps somewhat as follows:

"Your Honor, I offered to sublet the apartment for him and save him any trouble. I know that I could have gotten some nice desirable tenants for him. I knew I had signed a lease and was willing to make up for the fact that I had to leave before it was over. (Note: it will do no harm to avoid the term "breaking the lease.") I even had talked to some people who were interested, but Mr. ——— wouldn't even consider the matter and I don't feel that was very reasonable of him. Any trouble he went through he brought on himself; he didn't lose any rent—in fact he may have raised the rent." (or, if he did lose some rent: "he didn't have to lose any rent.") "Now, he's just keeping that extra month's rent as some sort of extra penalty." (Note: for reasons you will see below, it is a good thing to use the word "penalty.")

Short of calling you a liar, there's not much a landlord can say to this except point to the lease and quote its terms. He will probably also throw in damage to the apartment, or pull out a bill for repainting. Well, here is where the concept of normal wear and tear comes in. Ask him when the apartment was last painted, and why he hasn't got that record if it was only two years ago. The burden of proof for damages is on him.

If the judge doesn't accept this argument or you hadn't laid the proper groundwork to enable you to use it, you are still far from finished. Your fall-back argument is that the clause in the lease falls into the forbidden legal category of "penalty clause."

Perhaps the classic penalty clause of all time is the

infamous "pound of flesh" that Shylock was going to extract from Antonio because the ship did not get in on time. Perhaps the Italians have different legal notions, but you can't chop your debtor up in Massachusetts, or any of the other forty-nine states for that matter. That would be a "penalty," that is, a contract provision that requires the party who breaches the contract to pay the other party money or property or services or anything else whose value bears no relation to the damages actually caused by the breach. If the amount of money being withheld bears no relationship to the damages the landlord suffered as a result of your leaving, then the clause is a penalty clause and the law will tote up the damages according to its own rules.

On the other hand, there is something that is a close cousin to a penalty clause that is valid and permitted, the so-called "liquidated damages" clause. A liquidated damages clause comes into play in a situation where both parties acknowledge that a breach of a certain contract provision will result in damages that are real but difficult to "liquidate," that is, to pin a precise money figure to. So rather than waste time arguing later, the parties may agree to assign a reasonable value to them at the time the contract is signed. That, of course, is the interpretation the landlord's attorney is going to put on the clause.

Indeed, the clause itself will undoubtedly be headlined "liquidated damages" or have the phrase in it, and the lawyer will make a big show out of this. Don't let it bother you. The question of whether a clause is a penalty or liquidated damages clause is a question of law for the court to decide. The other side's self-serving characterization has zero weight. Just because they call a duck a swan, they don't bind the court to anything. And what you are going to argue is that if it walks like a duck, quacks like a duck, and acts like a duck, it's a duck. That is, you are going to argue that the clause in question has all the indicia of a penalty clause.

First you argue that the clause has no relation to the damages suffered. Did he lose any rent? If so, how much? How much time did he spend re-renting? The landlord may argue that he rented through an agent, which cost him a fee. Fine. Demand to see the receipt. Agent's fees are usually two weeks rent or less. If his is higher, demand why, and ask why he didn't let you rent it. (This is where the duty to mitigate damages, if it applies to leases, will come in.) If the landlord can show directly related out-of-pocket expenses, then you should of course be required to reimburse him. But he shouldn't get more. Or he may argue that his renting the apartment himself is worth the prevailing agent's fee. This is a reasonable argument and the judge may accept it, but this fee will probably not amount to your whole security deposit.

Your next argument that the clause is a penalty clause depends on the way the lease is drafted. Most leases provide something along the line that the security deposit will be returned "provided tenant is not in default in fully and faithfully performing all of the terms, conditions, and covenants contained herein." If that is the general character of the lease provision, you should point out that the landlord could have kept the deposit for any violation of the numerous conditions of the lease, no matter how minor. The longer the lease and thus the more covenants you could have run afoul of, the stronger this argument is.

Now, if the argument revolves around one of these if-you-leave-early-you-give-us-the-security-deposit clauses, a good landlord lawyer will make the argument that it is not a penalty clause, but an *option* to break the lease. You can reply that you thought an option was something you actually paid for in advance and that if this clause was really an option, it should have been headlined that way.

Your final argument is that if there is any doubt what this clause is, it should be characterized as a penalty clause because of the legal rule that ambiguities in contracts are to be decided against the drafter. This, of course, is a big advantage for you, because all you have to do is raise a doubt. Then the burden of proof is shifted to the other side to show unambiguously that it is a liquidated damages clause. If you have done your job right, this should be an impossible job for the other side to do.

One procedural point should be added here. One of the important lessons of this book has been that you are much better off if you eschew legal terms and argue your case in plain English, phrased in a way that makes it appear accidental that you have just made a shatteringly brilliant legal argument. Well, when you start talking about penalty clauses and liquidated damages, this particular jig is up. The stuff is at a sufficient level of legal sophistication to make the judge curious about where you got your legal knowledge. If he asks, tell the truth and direct him to the nearest bookstore. In any event, you will do well to preface your original remarks with protestations of legal ignorance. "Now Your Honor, I'm certainly not a lawyer and don't know much about these things, but from what I understand this thing is illegal because it's something called a penalty clause . . ." Do not underestimate the value of a little of this kind of mazola. Remember, you want to avoid turning on the little light in his head that says "wise guy" or "know-it-all."

Occasionally, you will be forced to move because something really bad goes wrong with your apartment and the landlord refuses to fix it. In a case like this, you usually have a choice between all-out war or graceful retreat. You can call the health department for an inspection, ask the local tenant's group to help you start a rent strike, or picket your landlord. Or, if you can afford the time and effort less than you can afford the cost of moving and were thinking of splitting that dump anyway, you can simply move.

If for some reason the landlord holds your deposit, you can of course sue him to get it back; indeed, you can even add the cost of moving. But I would definitely contact a lawyer, even if you seem justified in your action, before moving. You might have a case for greater damages or need him to lay the groundwork.

At any rate, if you do end up suing in Small Claims Court under such circumstances, you should keep in mind the five elements you are going to have to show in court:

1. Notice of Condition: You should have informed the landlord of the problem.

2. Demand for Repairs: You should stick this in with the notice.

3. Notice of Intention to Vacate: "If this can't be fixed within X days, I am simply going to be forced to leave."

4. Causal Connection between the Condition and Your Departure.

5. Documentation of Condition.

Here, all the standard techniques should be used. Letters sent certified mail, return receipt requested, records should be kept, and witnesses. Don't forget to inform the landlord of special damages you may be suffering, for example, danger to your tropical plant collection or your health. (But don't forget, either, your duty to mitigate damages.)

In court you will of course avoid the term "constructive eviction." If you point out that you were happy there but were "forced" to leave, the point should be pretty obvious.

Getting Back Your Security Deposit If You Don't Move In—the "Deposit to Hold."

Often enough to warrant comment, a situation arises where someone puts a deposit to "hold" an apartment for a couple of weeks until he or she is ready to move in, and then has a change of mind. If this happens to you, can you get some or all of the deposit back? Your legal position depends partly on the reasons for your change of mind, and partly on what was said at the time of the oral contract. If the deposit was given in return for a promise to hold the apartment for a specified period of time and the landlord remains willing and ready in good faith to do so and you simply changed your mind, then you are not in a very strong legal or moral position unless you can demonstrate some sort of substantial misstatement or a "hidden defect"—roaches, etc. On the other hand, when the sum you are giving up is disproportionate to the "damages" the landlord suffered—if, for example, he easily re-rented it—the reasoning and arguments of the previous section apply. And, if you were promised repairs or remodeling that were not forthcoming, then not only are you entitled to your money back, but you may deserve consequential damages for the moving trailer you rented and the hotel room you had to take while you were looking for a new apartment.

The points to keep in mind are:

1. What was said? Was the deposit to be returned? Was it taken only as compensation for holding the apartment or did he say that it would be applied to the first month's rent?

2. How soon after giving the deposit was the landlord notified? And how much time remained for him to rent the apartment?

3. Was the apartment in fact rented? Was another similar deposit taken?

4. What caused you to change your mind? Your own independent decision or a broken promise or hidden defect?

By the way, this is a situation where you might want to subpoena the eventual tenant as a witness. Since he or she will probably be reluctant to testify "against" a new landlord, you might be wise to subpoena first (getting the name off the mail box, if possible), then explaining that a notarized statement of the essential facts will do. That way, you will assure cooperation in getting the statement.

Getting Money From Landlords Whose Negligence Costs You Money.

Despite the fact that the law of landlord-tenant occupies its own special pigeonhole, one should not forget that other legal concepts also apply to the relationship, for example, negligence. If you live in a jurisdiction where the landlord has a duty to repair, for example, he is liable for the reasonably foreseeable consequences of that duty, as we have seen in the damages section.

Thus, if you notify a landlord of a defective condition, say a broken window lock, and he has time to repair it but doesn't and some burglar breaks in, you have strong grounds for a suit.

The elements of your case would be:

1. Notice to the landlord.

2. The passing of a "reasonable" amount of time between receipt of the notice and the event.

3. A causal connection between the loss and the negligence. If the burglar kicked the whole frame in, then there is less chance to collect, since the presence of the lock would presumably not have made much difference. (But was the window rotten and was this a condition the landlord should have known about?) The best way to establish the causal connection is by getting a copy of the police report, although your own testimony might suffice.

The landlord is also liable for personal injuries received on the premises owing to his negligence—the loose board, the dark hall. Once again, however, for virtually any kind of personal injury, your damages, including pain and suffering, are likely to be many times above the Small Claims Limit. See a lawyer.

By the way, if you sue the landlord for negligence, he is almost certain to be covered by insurance, so you should be prepared to deal with an insurance company lawyer and go through negotiations.

Finally, landlords have legitimate rights, too, and these can be exercised in SCC. If you are a small landlord and you are owed back rent or compensation for excessive damages to the apartment, SCC might be the best route for you. After all, guess whose property taxes are supporting it?

CHAPTER VIII

SCC REFORM—THE SEVEN NON-COMMANDMENTS

You may find this chapter boring and no help at all in the matter at hand. Sorry. On the other hand, there's absolutely no obligation to read it, nor any reason to unless you have become intrigued with the institution and its potential. As for me, the itch to put in my two cents' worth on how this particular segment of the cosmos should be ~~re-engineered was just too strong. I~~ just had to scratch.

It turns out that the first thing that happens to someone catapulted into the recommendation biz is an attack of the Ten Commandments syndrome. The temptation is to assume an omniscient posture and the imperative mode and to start filling up the old tablets with definitive statements on the way it should be.

There are two major problems with this approach. First, the concentration on the means tends to overshadow the ends in mind. Before people can evaluate suggestions on how to get there, they should know where they're going, and maybe even why. These last two are, after all, the major decisions. And understanding the basic blueprint makes for a more discerning debate over what kind of bricks to use.

The second problem is that the recommendation approach becomes too confining because of the nature of recommendations. As we all know, recommendations come in two species: grandiose and ungrandiose (also known as prosaic). Each kind has something to recommend it. Prosaic suggestions have the virtue of being eminently sensible, reasonable, and appealing to a broad segment of potential supporters. They are evolutionary rather than revolutionary. All of this respectability, however, makes them a bit like teetotalers: solid, but a trifle on the dull side at times. Committees make prosaic recommendations.

Grandoise recommendations, on the other hand, tend to involve more unrestrained leaps of the spirit, challenging old concepts and promoting attention-focusing dialogue. They are imaginative, sweeping, and groovy. Unfortunately, they tend to be a little hard to sell to the powers that be. Also, they cast a shadow over more prosaic recommendations that accompany them.

So what happens is that all these agonizing choices have to be made in assembling the optimally balanced recommendation portfolio—creative but not threatening, solid but not too timid.

Well, beans for that.

The cost of getting around these problems is merely taking a demotion, from Czar of the Universe issuing commandments, to Master Chef explicating recipes. Once a specific dish is agreed upon, the ingredients according to most recipes consist by and large of the same basic elements. The difference is in how one puts together the little of this and little of that, and perhaps in a few optional flourishes.

What I have tried to concoct is a strategic recipe for a b*st*rd-proof Small Claims Court—one where the talons of justice will cheaply and efficiently close on the malefactor and not unclutch until satisfaction has been rendered no matter how much the miserable scoundrel wriggles. The ingredients are the universal ones. The instructions consist of a basic philosophy for handling them, with explanations of details. As with any recipe, you may modify to taste, keeping in mind that the proof of the pudding is in the eating.

1. INGREDIENT: Lawyers.
   PHILOSOPHY: Eliminate.

Lawyers are the original sin of Small Claims Court. SCC is supposed to be a layman's court, a forum that eliminates judicial middlemen and all the lengthy technical wrangling associated with their presence. Lawyers in SCC inevitably behave in their accustomed mode, arguing over every possible point. After all, that is what they are hired to do. The problem is that all this sound and fury is mightily intimidating to mere mortals.

There is no need to tolerate this chilling effect on free and easy speech in Small Claims Court. The two fundamental justifications for introducing lawyer overhead into the justice-dispensing process do not apply here. In the adversary system, in which you have two sides battling simultaneously to build up their own cases and tear down the other side's, in the expectation that the truth will somehow out, lawyers, through their knowledge of substantive and procedural law: (1) structure the legal issues; (2) guide the proceedings through the maze of arcane technical rules that have grown up to safeguard the rights of the parties against unfair treatment; and (3) even out the odds in the case of adversaries of differing skill levels.

In Small Claims Court, because the claims are "small," the policy judgment has been made that the time and cost benefits of streamlining procedure outweigh the risk of attenuating these safeguards. There *are* no technical rules to speak of.

Not so easily dismissed is the lawyer's mostly out-of-court function in spotting and analyzing the legal issues involved. It has, I hope, been made abundantly clear in all sections of this book that the layman's lawbooks are no substitute for the skills a person trained in the law brings to these tasks. Those who wage and win their cases without lawyers under the present set-up seem to manage all right and there seems to be no reason why a plaintiff or defendant can't consult an attorney for the limited purpose of having the law outlined in general terms.

There is substantial doubt that lawyers are needed at all for this purpose. Lots of people who have studied the problem of Small Claims Court believe that this function can very effectively be served by non-lawyer SCC "advisors" who would work at the clerk's office and would be available to give advice to litigants in all phases of their case, perhaps assuming an informed conciliation role, and just being generally helpful. As time goes by, such an advisor would become familiar with many of the aspects of the law. All of this is already being tried in the recently opened Harlem branch of the New York City Small Claims Court.

One final note on the necessity for SCC litigants to know substantive law. There's something to be said for a situation in which the parties tell their stories without being overly encumbered with notions about what effect this or that statement will have on the case. The natural temptation to tailor facts is avoided. Given the emergence of a general set of facts and the power to cross-examine, an experienced judge is quite capable of applying relevant law with no help at all from the parties in this regard. Ignorance of the law may be felicitous to the true ends of justice in this case.

As for the lawyer's role in evening the odds between adversaries of uneven skills, this certainly is not the result when one party has a lawyer and the other does not (although the tendency of the judge to "represent" the other litigant in these circumstances somewhat mitigates the problem). It is probably a good working assumption that those who need this odds-evening service are generally poor people. The poor, however, because of their eligibility for legal aid, do have access to a lawyer (in fact, more access than the rest of us). And if Legal Aid attorneys decide that a case has merit but that the person involved would be unable to represent him or herself effectively, then there's no reason why the case cannot be brought in regular court.

About the only person whose legitimate interests might be hurt by banning lawyers from the court is the innocent defendant. (There really are some, you know.) After all, he didn't ask for all of this trouble. Why should he be made to traipse down to the courtroom, particularly if he is innocent? Why shouldn't he be allowed to send a lawyer? (I assume there's not much sense to making him go through the trouble of digging up a non-lawyer to send.) I think we can give this guy a fair deal, but that the way to do it is by the proper structuring of transfer provisions, as you shall see if you forge ahead.

But, as far as allowing lawyers in Small Claims Court, although lawyers do lots of good things and perform many useful functions (If they didn't, there wouldn't be so many of them, now would there?), arguing cases in Small Claims Court is not one of them.

2. INGREDIENT: Escape mechanisms—transfer and appeal.
   PHILOSOPHY: Allow if need be,
   but make option unattractive.

Basically, the more it can be assured that what is started in Small Claims Court will end there—and quickly—the more meaningful will be the right to use it. The same considerations that justified the partial elision of due process safeguards by simplified procedure also argue for limiting the avenues of escape from the forum and appeal from its determination.

The problems in implementing this policy are more constitutional than conceptual. You can't just issue an edict saying "no transfer, no appeal" because this would take away rights guaranteed by the Constitution.

For the plaintiff, the problem is relatively simple. He is given notice that by his choosing to use Small Claims Court instead of regular court, he automatically waives the right to appeal.

As for the defendant, the illegality of depriving him of appeal rights can be avoided by giving a transfer option, that is, letting him remove the case to regular court before trial. The problem with this approach by itself is that it would make Small Claims Court useless against anyone who decided to hire a lawyer. Remember, we have excluded lawyers from the court. What would happen is that anytime a corporation, retailer, landlord, or savvy defendant was sued, he would merely hire a lawyer, who would transfer the case. This would: (1) cause additional delay, and (2) make the plaintiff hire his own lawyer or be ground into legal hamburger as he tried to present his own case in regular court.

Three alternatives are available to head off this situation. One is not to allow transfer and to make appeal from Small Claims Court bothersome enough to discourage it. The second would be to allow transfer, but to require the person requesting the transfer to reimburse the other party for attorney's fees if the other party prevails.

This second alternative does three things: (1) it certainly reduces the guilty defendant's incentive to remove the case. Some time may be saved, but the cost will be high; (2) it takes a great deal of the burden off the plaintiff. He can leave the legal driving to the lawyer, not to mention any post-judgment bloodhounding that might be needed to collect; and (3) it solves the little problem of the busy innocent defendant we had a couple of pages ago. He can just hire a lawyer, which will cost him less than the value he puts on the time the matter would otherwise take.

The third alternative, which may or may not be constitutionally permissible, would be to allow a plaintiff who has been transferred to a regular court to choose to have Small Claims Court simplified procedural rules apply. On balance, I prefer the second alternative.

3. INGREDIENT: Jurisdictional limit.
   PHILOSOPHY: Keep small except against
                 those with deep pockets.

I think that $500 is a good claim limit in ordinary circumstances, because anything more than that can really hurt. Not only the defendant that loses, but the plaintiff that deserves the money but blows his case because he depended on this book or a bar room lawyer instead of getting competent representation. Anything below the $500 is not going to send anyone to the poorhouse, and once you get above that the cost of a lawyer's services becomes economically justifiable.

The argument for higher limits is that a very large proportion of consumer complaints come in a few categories of purchases involving sums generally over the limit—cars and major appliances being the most obvious examples.

The assumption is that these defendants have what lawyers lovingly refer to as deep pockets—ability to pay—and there is less tendency to sympathize with their vulnerability to larger judgments.

I think that on balance, notwithstanding the increased penalty for pro se plaintiff incompetence, it does make sense to raise limits in automobile and appliance categories. Here is a case where opening up the courts in this manner has a good chance of having a direct effect on the quality of consumer goods in this country.

As a matter of fact, as a housekeeping and publicity matter, I would create special branches of the court just to hear automobile and appliance sales cases, with limits of maybe $3000 and $1000 respectively. I think the existence of these separate branches (in reality, just differently scheduled sessions), would spur both public awareness of the opportunity to use them and the development of better laws protecting consumers, as well as promoting the dissemination of materials explaining warrantee rights in understandable language.

4. INGREDIENT: Collection.

PHILOSOPHY: Instant repay.

As we have seen, a judgment is something less than cash in hand; and converting it into such can be the biggest hassle of the whole Small Claims process. For this most difficult problem of all, the solution is the most simple: let the government put its money where its mouth is. For Small Claims Court, the judgment-is-a-hunting-license principle should be dumped and replaced by a system whereby the court pays the winner and takes it upon itself to collect from the loser. Besides assuring that the trial has not been an empty charade, the method makes procedural sense because it is easier for a governmental unit both to track people down and to shake them down. If too many judgment debtors are slipping through the net, there is a vested interest to improve the process, since any lost revenues will come out of the court's budget.

Human nature being what it is, it seems to me this policy of providing instant financial gratification would do more than any other single reform to popularize the court and to restore a measure of confidence in the effectiveness of the judicial process. There's no reason that the complaint to collection time couldn't be reduced to three or four weeks, an incredible contrast to regular courts and current experience in SCC.

I would make only one exemption to this policy, namely for default judgments. There is simply too much risk that substantial justice is not being done in these cases even if corporate plaintiffs are largely barred from the court. In this case, I would require service of notice of default and the consequences and give the defaulter one last chance to appear in court. If he fails to appear, or appears and loses, then payment would be made, and the hounds of Legalville would be loosed upon him.

5. INGREDIENT: Good judges and long-range supervision of the court.

   PHILOSOPHY: Do as Chairman Mao would do: Let the judges go before the people.

There are indications that we are entering the biggest era of Chinoiserie since the period the term refers to—the French Court of the eighteenth century. (The term basically means that some segment of the society goes ga-ga over Chinese culture and attempts to explore it by bastardized emulations of various sorts.)

We could do worse. Anyone who has done what Old Man Mao has done since the Long March has to be a pretty shrewd fortune cookie in my book. I respect his judgment as a policy maker, and think that there might be a thing or two we can learn from the Chinese about running things.

One of the soundest principles he has espoused, it seems to me, is sending the bureaucrats back to the fields. Nothing like a little contact between the peasants and the mandarins to establish perspective from both sides.

Of course, the Chinese are lucky enough to have fields to send people back to; we are not quite set up the same way. Luckily, we are not talking about literal interpretation, but policy emulation, applying the basic principles to our situation. And in this regard, it's certainly not too far-fetched to consider Small Claims Courts the judicial "fields" (and "laymen" plaintiffs the legal "peasants").

Therefore, if I were running things, I would require that each judge, no matter what his hierarchical rank, spend, oh, two weeks to a month in Small Claims Court every year. The benefits from this would be severalfold.

First of all, it would probably assure a high degree of fairness in the judging, since even the most autocratic curmudgeon is generally on his best behavior in Small Claims Court for various psychological reasons. Also, it would seem to me an automatic watchdog device both on how the courts are run and on spotting areas where the law is unfair to ordinary persons and needs changing. (After all, that's one of the functions of judges— to "make" law.) A little feedback can go a long way.

And for the judges, it would be a welcome change of pace, certainly no more burdensome than, say, National Guard summer camp or military reserve meetings, especially since it is no added drain on their time.

Actually, once you start thinking about the possibilities involved here, lots of dandy grandiose recommendations present themselves. Add in the related devolution-of-power notion of "decentralization" and you come up with the notion of reviving "circuit courts." Originally, a circuit court was a judge on horseback going around to where the judging was needed. Why not Small Claims Courtmobiles going into local communities and holding court right there in front of the little city hall, or branch of the public library (where suits could also be filed). Those communities unwilling to raise the property tax to buy a Courtmobile can pay taxi fare to send the judge to a local public building, although a certain amount of publicity value is thereby lost.

Incidentally, it seems to me that *all* judges should be

required to do this, right up to the Supreme Court level. The way it stands, this really wouldn't be possible for federal judges, since there are no federal courts with the exception of the Washington, D.C. Small Claims Court, which is technically a branch of the Supreme Court itself. One theoretical solution would be to create a federal Small Claims Court, and it's not a bad practical idea, particularly in the area of tax and other areas where citizens deal with bureaucrats, such as pension disputes. The other solution is to put Warren Burger in Small Claims Court once in a while (something to which he might well cheerfully acquiesce, since he appears genuinely interested in the problem of court reform).

At any rate, there is no reason why we shouldn't take advantage of the potential Small Claims Courts have for keeping judges in touch with the day-to-day legal concerns of the people. This is certainly a desirable ingredient even in determinations of the most esoteric points of law. After all who does the law belong to?

6. INGREDIENT: Arbitration.
   PHILOSOPHY: Use the mandatory optional system.

As we have seen, an arbitration session is a court of non-law in which an impartial third party sits down with the disputants and sees if he can help them come to a settlement. An arbitrator has at once absolute power in that he can propose any damn fool settlement that seems like a good idea at the time—and no power whatsoever in that his decision cannot be imposed upon the parties without their consent. Arbitration is thus more flexible than regular courts, but not without its own limits.

In practice, it is also less formal than court, typically consisting of the parties sitting alone around a table in a little room with an arbitrator dressed in civies. The biggest practical advantage of injecting arbitration into the Small Claims Court process is its time-saving function, which makes it possible for backlogs to be kept down to a minimum even in very busy courts. In New York City, for example, where arbitration by volunteer lawyers is heavily relied upon, four or five times as many cases will be settled in an evening as could have been without arbitrators. And as a result, waiting time is surprisingly short in that otherwise legally congested city.

The one difference between arbitration and regular court session that I saw and that was confirmed in interviews and in a study of the New York City Small Claims Court system is that arbitrators are "somewhat more prone to compromise." Well, life is much more prone to produce situations in which neither disputant has a monopoly on justice. I'm half okay, you're half okay.

Arbitration thus turns out to be an unequivocally sensible, time-saving idea; and there's little question but that it belongs in any SCC system where backlogs would otherwise accumulate. It's also a dandy volunteer job for all those lawyers who are going to be heartbroken because they are not otherwise able to make a contribution to the workings of SCC. Therefore, to dig up arbitrators, I would put the arm on the local bar association, reminding them of the grand tradition of *pro bono publico* work and the fact that judges like to go home early, too, and get grouchy when they can't, particularly at lawyers who had better things to do than volunteer their services in SCC arbitration.

The only question is to what extent the arbitration should be left optional. In New York, the litigants make a pre-trial choice on trial day between arbitration and going before the judge. Those who choose arbitration are bound by what the arbitrator decides. (Theoretically, I have seen an arbitrator confronted by a strenuously objecting party withdraw and suggest they take it to the judge. They did and the crybaby lost.)

The New York system works pretty well, but arbitrators note that they still feel somewhat compelled to reach only decisions justifiable by fairly formal applications of legal rules.

I think I would set it up a trifle differently. I would make appearance before an arbitrator for a ten-minute session mandatory; but the decision of the arbitrator would be on an optional "take-it-or-leave-it" basis. Both arbitrators and litigants would be told that although the arbitrator is a lawyer and will take the principles of the law into account when reaching his suggested settlement, he is not bound by the law in the same way that the judge is and many of his decisions will be compromises in situations where the law would dictate more one-sided results. If either party felt they deserved more, then the case would go before the judge; but the parties would be warned that the case will then be decided "by the book" with the chips falling where they may.

In practice this system, although interesting, might prove too cumbersome if too many cases got sent to the judge. In that case, I would either get more persuasive arbitrators or switch to the New York City system.

7. INGREDIENT: Various little touches.
   PHILOSOPHY: They can make or break
                the cake—do them right.

There are some miscellaneous small, but important parts of the overall recipe:

1. Court sessions should be scheduled so people don't have to lose time from work. This means evenings and weekends.

2. In many jurisdictions, businesses must be sued under their technical name, discovering them involves a trip to the county clerk or secretary of state's office. This is nonsensical. Small Claims Court suits should be permitted in "DBA" names, that is against defendants as listed on their door, letterhead, or advertisements.

3. Lots of violations of rights occur against the eighteen-to-twenty group. Old enough to vote, old enough to sue. The minimum plaintiff age should be no greater than eighteen. As a matter of fact, I see no reason why anyone at, say, high school junior level or above, should not be allowed to sue the court if the occasion arises.

4. Summonses and other forms are extraordinarily confusing to the layman. Special Small Claims Court forms in clear English (with Spanish translation where needed) should be adopted.

So that's all folks. But I think it would be enough to produce a practical, inexpensive, just, court system that would serve about 200 million.

CHAPTER IX

IN PRAISE OF SPITE AND FURY

There is nothing wrong with Faith, Hope, or Charity. In moderation, each has its place in the scheme of things, and the world would undoubtedly be a better place if there were more of each around. (If the impossible is accomplished, the unattainable can always be achieved.)

Nevertheless, when it comes to the nitty-gritty things that a Small Claims case is made of, I'll trade away pounds of the cardinal virtues any day for an ounce or so of that vastly underestimated quality—spite.

Spite is a highly uncharitable form of anger that we are all supposed to repress because it's not very nice. The problem with that approach is that if you go around being nice all the time, the world is going to make a meatball out of you. If you are understanding, uncomplaining, and accepting of things, I don't think you are going to inherit the earth at all. The basic psychological laws of the universe being what they are, I think you are more likely to develop a migraine and pass the bad vibes on. You are going to end up taking it out by kicking the cat, withholding sex from your spouse, driving your car like a boor, or just generally walking around with a face that would stop an eight-day clock.

Better you should sue. You've been inconvenienced; you've lost time and money; you've been frazzled; now let's see how they like it. And if you do sue and are lucky, you are going to get to a point in your adventures when a wave of joyful calm engulfs your feelings on the case, a point where the specific facts involved no longer matter, where the money no longer matters, where, as a matter of fact, nothing seems to matter very much any longer except the sweet nectar of seeing your civil right vindicated. You will have surpassed spite and achieved existential fury. And then those b*st*rds better watch out, because existential fury is superfly stuff.

It is fitting that we close with the inspirational tale of one man who has made one of the largest corporations in the world feel the heat of his existential fury and become very, very sorry about it. The plaintiff in what surely must be the greatest Small Claims Court case of the twentieth century, thus far, is named Robert Warren and lives on the East Side of New York, where he runs a number of small and imaginative literary enterprises from his residence.

Like many other members of modern society, Warren is telephone dependent. (He has three lines and several extensions.) If the phone doesn't work, if he can't get his call through, if the circuit is busy, if he has to re-dial the number four times, if he can't get a dial tone, he is losing time, and therefore money. And what's more important, stomach lining. Dialing a telephone number four times is a hassle. For years, as the telephone service in midtown New York deteriorated, the minute annoyances of each faulty phone call accumulated, accumulated, accumulated, like space dust falling on the moon. Because of the growing unreliability of phone service, it was just becoming less and less fun to work and live the way he was used to. This frustration, of course, was being simultaneously experienced by millions of other New Yorkers—not to mention Bostonians, Los Angelinos, San Franciscans, Chicagoans, etc. Some of them, including the New York City Department of Consumer Affairs, had even tried to take Ma Bell to court to force the improvement of service, but the law is very loathe to issue court orders of such a general nature, and the suits came to naught.

Warren was not the first to sue. But he was the first to sue in Small Claims Court. It began with a New Year's resolution on January 1, 1970, the day he got tired of being a meatball and vowed to keep detailed records of the time lost because of the abysmal telephone service in New York City.

He put a logbook beside his phone and used the ordinary wasted time to build a record of exactly how much time the lousy service was costing him. Thirty seconds here, a minute and a half there, two minutes there, for waiting for a dial tone, waiting for operators to answer or information to answer, or waiting for information supervisors to take over after the regular information operators were unable to locate numbers which were clearly in their records, and a variety of other types of service inadequacies that we are all perhaps too familiar with. At the end of eight months, his little ledger toted up to a somewhat astounding 61¼ wasted, frustrating, miserable hours.

We saw sometime back that you generally cannot collect for lost time, no matter how infuriating. This was somewhat different in two respects. First of all, it could arguably be considered wages lost, since most of this time was consumed when Warren was using the phone for business purposes. Secondly, it could be considered a suit for damages for breach of contract. Warren's argument was that he was not receiving the benefit of his bargain with the phone company, in that he was "promised" in the law a reasonable level of phone service, that he was paying for such a level, that the constant hassles needed to get through to the other party constituted a less than reasonable level of service, that since he was dealing with a public monopoly he had to accept that level of service, but that he was entitled to be compensated for the extra effort (in this case, time) spent by him in order to obtain the service he had been promised.

Based on this reasoning, he sent the phone company a bill for his time, computed at a modest writer-researcher rate of five dollars per hour, for a total of $306.25.

Naturally, Ma Bell took the letter somewhat less than seriously, and did not exactly hasten to write out the check. As things turned out, she'd have been much better off to pay him. When it became plain that he was not about to get the money, Warren then filed suit as a $306.25 creditor of the American Telephone and Telegraph Company.

Then the fun began.

First, there were two continuances, which was a shame, since Warren, who is hardly a press-relations neophyte, had the grandstands packed with reporters. At any rate, things got rolling the third time.

Warren had brought his ledger along and gave a sample reading, then offered it to the court with the unpaid bill he had sent, and rested his case.

After a desultory cross-examination, the telephone company attorney got down to legal business.

His first argument was the one about Warren's time not being compensable. He claimed that for Warren to be paid for his time would amount to the same thing as paying somebody for the time spent going to and from work, waiting for a train, or waiting in the doctor's office.

At this point Judge Bentley Kassal intervened, reminding the lawyer that he could take another train or find another doctor, but that New York Telephone was the only game in town. The lawyer then shifted gears, claiming that the N.Y. State Public Service Commission, and not the Court, had jurisdiction over the matter, a technical argument at best.

Well, if he was going to get technical so was the judge. His Honor asked him for chapter-and-verse citations. The lawyer admitted that he had none with him, but said he'd send them.

The judge recessed the proceedings to give the telephone company lawyer a chance to submit the citations. When the phone company's brief came in a couple of weeks later, Warren took the trouble to go look up the cases cited.

And as he read the cases actually cited by the telephone company's attorney, he noticed one difference between them and his suit; the cases cited were all based on complaints about the level of service the phone company was giving, or were class actions. An important element in each of these cases was the demand for improved service. Warren's suit, however, made no such demand. He was just arguing about recovering a fair payment for time lost. He was perfectly willing to accept the atrocious level of service provided by the phone company. He just wanted compensation for the time and effort he had had to spend to make up for the fact that it wasn't up to snuff. Thus, those cases did not apply to his situation.

In order to take care of the jurisdictional question, he merely wrote a letter to the State Public Service Commission asking whether they had jurisdiction in the matter of a bill sent to the telephone company for money due for time and services rendered. He requested an immediate reply and received a letter stating that, indeed, although the question might well turn on the precise facts underlying the dispute, the P.S.C. did not have jurisdiction in ordinary circumstances to render money judgments for services rendered utilities otherwise subject to its jurisdiction.

Warren wrote up his conclusions, submitted his own "brief" to the court, along with the letter from the Public Service Commission, and waited for a decision.

When it came down, it must have ruined somebody's day over at New York Telephone. Judge Kassal issued what he called an "interim" decision. Basically, what the decision said was, "Okay, phone company, start talkin' and make it convincing, cause you're gonna have to talk your way out of this one."

First, the judge found as a matter of law that the telephone company had an obligation to furnish services that were "adequate, efficient, and proper." However, because of the telephone company's rules and regulations (which had been filed with and approved by the P.S.C.), the company was not liable for damages arising from delays and errors and inadequate, inefficient or improper services in the absence of "gross negligence and willful misconduct." In other words the phone company, writing its own laws, had insulated itself from liability.

What Judge Kassal said, however, was that in view of the evidence submitted by Warren, the burden of proof had shifted to the telephone company to show that it was not grossly negligent in the service it had provided to him. Therefore, the judge ruled that a regular trial would be held on this issue, with the phone company expected to prove its non gross negligence.

The story of that trial would be a book in itself. At this point, Warren got himself a few volunteer lawyers and the proceedings began in September, continued in an uneven schedule until the next April and resulted in over two thousand pages of briefs, testimony, and statements.

Warren sought to place in issue the service of the entire telephone company, but for purposes of the trial the evidence was limited to his own exchange, Midtown Manhattan, and the operation of the telephone equipment at the East 56th Street Central Office. This was the phone facility that was supposed to be servicing all the new skyscrapers that were being built during the East Side New York building boom of the late Sixties.

It turned out that because of what the court ultimately called the phone company's "negligence," in not planning for any of the tremendous increase of demand this was going to entail, the telephone wires in that Central Office had grown into an incredible snarl that was almost impossible for repairmen to work on. The main wiring frame looked like the estate of the world's biggest string collector. The phone company had even had to invent a special tool to work with the wires on the overloaded wiring board, a rather odd way to face the problem when you think about it. What it boiled down to was that no one could get a call through in New York City because the phone company had been too stupid to foresee increased demand. (One of the high points of the battle, was a picture of this tangled mess, called the "spaghetti picture," by Judge Kassal, which friendly forces delivered to Warren out of the telephone company files, and which was introduced successfully into evidence.) Another aspect of the case that Warren still finds particularly interesting was the amazing prescience with which the phone company seemed to anticipate legal maneuvers that had been discussed by Warren and his colleagues over the phone.

To make a long story short, Warren has not yet received his money. But the court ruled that the phone company was not "grossly negligent," since somewhere along the line they had begun to take some fumbling steps to improve service. The judge found against Warren, and he still has not collected his $306.25. (He is however mapping his appeal plans at this very moment.)

Even if the Supreme Court decides against him, Warren at least has the satisfaction of knowing that he made the world's largest corporation scramble, and in so doing, played a big part in getting the entire East Side of New York unscrambled. A lot of people spend a lifetime accomplishing considerably less.

How many other problems are susceptible to the "Warren Gambit"? Take your gripe, turn it into a money claim, and sue for damages. Who knows? It depends on judges sympathetic and imaginative enough to entertain creative lawsuits at that level; it depends on journalists aggressive and resourceful enough to publicize interesting cases; it depends on spreading a little knowledge around on people's civil rights; but most of all it depends on you and me and the guy down the street developing sufficient existential fury to follow through on our gripes about lousy services, lousy goods, lousy business practices, and whatever else is meatballing up.

The laws are on the books, and Small Claims Courts are waiting. We live in a Capitalist system; if we make it more expensive to provide lousy goods and services than good ones the market will "adjust." And, if enough of us start sticking up for our rights by complaining effectively and suing determinedly, it will become less expensive to sell quality than to sell junk. Don't kick the cat. Sue the B*st*rds. See you in court.

SCC INFORMATION
STATE-BY-STATE

What follows is a compendium of the core information on the Small Claims Court or equivalent system of each of the fifty states, the District of Columbia, Puerto Rico, and the Virgin Islands. Because of the diversity of such systems throughout the country and rapidly changing SCC legislation, compiling this information has not been the simple mechanical task one might assume it to be. There are many idiosyncratic wrinkles from place to place; statutes are often fragmented and unclear; and even the most conscienscious and cooperative court personnel have gaps in their knowledge and come up with contradictory answers to various questions.

Nevertheless, from analysis of every state statute, telephone research, checking the few relevant studies that have been done, and making a reasonable assumption or two, it has been possible to assemble an information outline for each state. You can be reasonably confident of its accuracy since it is the most reliable information that best efforts by skilled researchers can provide; but the picture is changing fast and it is possible that some of the information will be dated by the time you read this.

Chances are, however, that this information will remain accurate for some time. And until someone goes to the considerable trouble of putting together something better, this is the place to begin to get a fix on the SCC set-up in your state.

By this stage, if the book has done its job, most of the material in the appendix should be self-explanatory; but here is a quick run-down on what each information category contains.

TYPE OF COURT

In order to give you a basic orientation to your state's system, the courts we are interested in have been divided into the following species:

1. Small Claims Courts per se: this is the largest category, consisting of those Small Claims Courts consciously established as such as a result of the reform movement earlier this century. Usually, they are special sessions of the regular municipal or district courts, which means that they are held at the regular courthouse. Generally, this type is characteristic of the Northeast, West Coast, and populist Midwest. These courts process the bulk of small claims cases handled in this country, and it is from observation of these courts that most of the points in this book were developed.

2. Justice of the Peace Courts: this is one of the oldest category of judicial office, and although on the wane, JP Courts form the second largest category. They are concentrated in the South, but also scattered through the Midwest and South West. They are essentially informal tribunals of petty jurisdiction often conducted by a non-lawyer who is elected or appointed. (JP Courts usually have minor criminal powers, such as prosecuting traffic violators.) So-called "Magistrate" courts are essentially the same species of tribunal under a different name. Although the rules of evidence and other procedural accoutrements often technically apply in these tribunals, they are rarely enforced.

3. Miscellaneous: the third category is a miscellany of arrangements—hybird, conciliation, dual jurisdiction, etc. Anything particularly important needed to understand these systems is explained under the COMMENTS section.

CLAIM LIMIT

A simple statement of the maximum amount for which you can sue as of early 1973. There is no minimum.

AGE LIMIT

The minimum age at which suit can be initiated without being accompanied by a parent or other adult. Usually, this is the same as the age of majority in the state.

FILING FEES

What it will cost you to file your claim; also, where available, what it will cost to have process served.

SERVICE OF PROCESS

The manner in which the defendant may be summoned to court. Sometimes it can be done by mail, sometimes only by a sheriff or marshal, and sometimes by any disinterested party.

VENUE

This is geographical distribution. A defendant must be sued in the court of proper venue, usually within the jurisdictional division that encompasses his residence or place of business. Sometimes, however, a plaintiff can sue in the district in which *he* resides, or even anyplace where he can serve the defendant. This can be more convenient for him and less so for the defendant, and thus an element of strategy.

NORMAL WAITING TIME

In many instances, reasonable estimate of the amount of time that normally elapses between initiation of suit and trial was obtainable; if so, it is listed.

ARBITRATION SYSTEM

As has been noted, some Small Claims Court systems have provisions for voluntarily having the case heard before arbitrators, or before the clerk acting as arbitrator, etc. If there is such a procedure in your jurisdiction, its features are described here.

LAWYERS

Some Small Claims Courts bar or limit lawyers. Others require them to appear in certain circumstances. Any such provisions are noted here.

CORPORATIONS

Many jurisdictions have provisions of various sorts abridging the rights of corporations to use the court. These provisions, if any, are here explained.

TRANSFER

Some jurisdictions allow the defendant to transfer the case to regular court. Often, this is simply used by defendants as a delaying tactic. Sometimes, the right of transfer is given in lieu of the right to appeal. Please note that in all jurisdictions, a counterclaim by the other side in excess of the jurisdictional limit will result in transfer of the case.

APPEAL

In some jurisdictions, appeal from Small Claims Courts is allowed, usually on posting of an appeal bond and other rigamarole. Please note that such appeal generally violates the spirit of SCC and is generally not such a hot idea anyway.

STATUTE OF LIMITATIONS

Most state Statutes of Limitations for civil action vary according to the cause of action. Torts limitations, for example, are often different from those of contracts, and some tort limitations differ from each other. Generally speaking, you will be instituting your action well within any of the statutes, but the range in each state has been indicated. One interesting pattern is that actions for injury to property usually have longer limitations than those for injuries for persons.

COMMENTS

A miscellany of useful additional information sometimes including addresses and phone numbers of courts.

ALASKA

TYPE: Small Claims.

CLAIM LIMIT: $1000.

MINIMUM AGE: 18.

STATUTE OF LIMITATIONS: 2–6 years.

FILING FEES: $5 plus $10 for personal service or $2.03 for registered mail.

NORMAL WAITING TIME: Two weeks. Date set at the time the answer is due.

SERVICE OF PROCESS: Personal or registered mail.

VENUE: Judicial district in which defendant resides.

ARBITRATION SYSTEM: None.

LAWYERS: Corporation must be represented by an attorney. Others may have attorney but not required to.

CORPORATIONS: May appear as plaintiff or defendant but must be represented by an attorney.

TRANSFER: District Court judge uses discretion to decide if a case should be heard as small claims or in regular District Court of concurrent jurisdiction. Cases are transferable by statute if an important or unusual point of law.

APPEAL: Appeal may be taken to the Superior Court on claims of greater than $50. Appeal must be taken within 30 days. Superior Court may choose to give a full new trial (trial de novo).

COMMENTS: The Small Claims Court is a special session of the District Court held at the discretion of the District Court judges.

ALABAMA

TYPE: Justice Courts (see comment).

CLAIM LIMIT: $300.

MINIMUM AGE: 21.

STATUTE OF LIMITATIONS: 1–6 years.

FILING FEES: $10 plus service.

NORMAL WAITING TIME: Trial date at discretion of Justice—may vary widely.

SERVICE OF PROCESS: Personal by sheriff or constable.

VENUE: Precinct where defendant resides.

ARBITRATION SYSTEM: None.

LAWYERS: Lawyers may appear but not required.

CORPORATIONS: May appear as plaintiff or defendant with or without attorney.

TRANSFER: No provision.

APPEAL: Appeal must be taken within five days. Payment of a $6 fee is required plus posting of a bond amounting to double the judgment plus costs.

COMMENTS: There are not "Small Claims" courts as such in Alabama. Prior to January 1, 1972, Justice of the Peace courts heard cases on claims involving less than $100. New legislation provided that after that date "Justice Courts" would hear all cases currently pending before Justice of the Peace courts and new cases involving claims less than $300. Statutes provide that the Justice courts have printed forms for use in the justice courts available for the convenience of the public.

ARIZONA

TYPE: Justice of the Peace—Superior.

CLAIM LIMIT: Justice of the Peace Courts have original jurisdiction on claims less than $200 and concurrent jurisdiction with the Superior Court on claims between $200 and $500. There is currently a proposed constitutional amendment to raise original jurisdiction to $500 and concurrent from $500 to $1000.

MINIMUM AGE: 21.

STATUTE OF LIMITATIONS: 1–4 years.

FILING FEES: Under $50: $1; over $50: $3. Plus service fee of five cents per mile counted one way and limited to 35 miles in both cases.

NORMAL WAITING TIME: Often several months.

SERVICE OF PROCESS: Sheriff.

VENUE: (a) actions against persons who contract debts and obligations and then move may be brought in any precinct where the defendant may be found; (b) action for collection of an account, enforcement of a contract or any other claim may be brought where the transaction was entered into or where the defendant lives at the option of the plaintiff.

ARBITRATION SYSTEM: No.

LAWYERS: Corporations must be represented. Other parties may have attorney but not required.

CORPORATIONS: Corporations may appear as plaintiff or defendant but corporations must be represented by an attorney.

TRANSFER: Claim may be removed if defendant files cross complaint greater than $500.

APPEAL: May appeal to Superior Court if claim greater than $20. Appellant must give notice of appeal at time of judgment or written notice within 5 days. Within 10 days, person appealing must post a bond of double the amount in contention and pay a $20 fee. Within 20 days a $4 fee must also be paid.

COMMENTS: Rules governing the Superior Court in Arizona also apply to Justice of the Peace Courts.

ARKANSAS

TYPE: Justice of the Peace—Mayor—Municipal.

CLAIM LIMIT: Justice of the Peace Courts: Contract and replevin (actions to regain an object) actions less than $200. Personal injury claims less than $100; Municipal Courts: under $500.

MINIMUM AGE: Males 21; Females 18.

STATUTE OF LIMITATIONS: 1–5 years.

FILING FEES: $3.50.

NORMAL WAITING TIME: 30 days.

SERVICE OF PROCESS: Constable or sheriff or deputy may make in hand service or leave at defendant's last and usual place of abode.

VENUE: Township where at least one of defendants resides.

ARBITRATION SYSTEM: No.

LAWYERS: Preferred by judge but not required for any party.

CORPORATIONS: May appear as plaintiff or defendant with or without lawyer.

TRANSFER: No provision.

APPEAL: May appeal to Circuit Court for trial de novo. Arkansas Statutes 26–1302 require filing of affidavit that appeal is not taken for delay, filing within 30 days, and posting of bond with one or more securities approved by the justice.

CALIFORNIA

TYPE: Small Claims.

CLAIM LIMIT: $500.

MINIMUM AGE: 21. 18 if married.

STATUTE OF LIMITATIONS: 1–4 years.

FILING FEES: $2 plus $1.50 for mail to each defendant.

NORMAL WAITING TIME: From 2 to 8 weeks depending on the location. In some cities the required waiting time depends on residency. In San Francisco residents must usually wait around 4 weeks and non-residents around 8. In Los Angeles, the trial usually comes up in less than a month for residents and 4 to 6 weeks for non-residents.

SERVICE OF PROCESS: Registered mail.

VENUE: (a) in action for breach of obligation undertaken, either in the judicial district or city or county where obligation undertaken was to have been performed or where the defendant resided at the institution of the action;

(b) in action for injury, in the judicial district where the injury occurred or where the defendant resides;

(c) in all other cases, where the defendant resides.

ARBITRATION SYSTEM: No.

LAWYERS: Attorneys are barred from the Small Claims Court.

CORPORATIONS: Corporations may appear as plaintiff or defendant but without an attorney.

TRANSFER: The case may be transferred before trial if defendant makes a counterclaim over $500.

APPEAL: Appeal is available only to the defendant. Appeal must be taken within 30 days of entry of judgment and a deposit or bond equal to the judgment plus $25 must be made. If defendant loses on appeal, he/she must pay costs plus a $15 attorney's fee to the plaintiff.

COMMENTS: California Small Claims Courts are among the best run in the country.

San Francisco Court: Room 303, City Hall, Van Ness Avenue, Ph. 558-3211

Los Angeles area courts:

Alhambra, 200 W. Woodward Ave., Alhambra, Cal., 289-6100

Antelope, 1040 W. Ave. J, Lancaster, Cal., 948-4615

Beverly Hills, 9355 Burton Way, Beverly Hills, Cal., 272-9681

Burbank, 399 E. Olive Ave., Burbank, Cal., 849-3353

Citrus, 1427 W. Service Ave., West Covina, Cal., 686-1010

Compton, 212 S. Acacia St., Compton, Cal., 639-6010

Culver, 4130 Overland Ave., Culver City, Cal., 870-7462

Downey, 8206 E. Third St., Downey, Cal., 773-0491

East Los Angeles, 4837 E. Third St., Los Angeles, Cal., 264-4200

El Monte, 11301 E. Valley Blvd., El Monte, Cal., 283-6416

Glendale, 600 E. Broadway, Glendale, Cal., 245-1831

Inglewood, 110 E. Regent St., Inglewood, Cal., 678-1241

Long Beach, 415 W. Ocean Blvd., Long Beach, Cal., 432-0411

Los Angeles, 110 N. Grand Ave., Los Angeles, Cal., 6-1551 or 6-1552

Los Cerritos, 10025 E. Flower St., Bellflower, Cal., 866-7011

Pasadena, 200 N. Garfield Ave., Pasadena, Cal., 861-4281

Pomona, 350 W. Fifth Ave., Pomona, Cal., 629-4171

San Antonio, 6548 Miles Ave., Huntington Park, Cal., 583-1751

Santa Anita, 300 W. Maple Ave., Monrovia,
Cal., 359-2581

Santa Monica, 1725 Main St., Santa Monica,
Cal., 451-5911

South Bay, 825 Maple Ave., Torrance, Cal.,
320-6010

South Gate, 8640 California Ave., South Gate,
Cal., 567-1341

Whittier, 7339 S. Painter Ave., Whittier, Cal.,
698-6251

COLORADO

TYPE: Small Claims (County Courts).

CLAIM LIMIT: $500.

MINIMUM AGE: 18.

STATUTE OF LIMITATIONS: 1–6 years.

FILING FEES: $7.

NORMAL WAITING TIME: 10 to 20 days.

SERVICE OF PROCESS: By registered mail or personal service by a disinterested person over 18.

VENUE: In city or county where the obligation in question was to be performed or where the defendant lives.

ARBITRATION SYSTEM: None.

LAWYERS: May appear for any party but required for corporation.

CORPORATIONS: May appear for plaintiff or defendant but required for corporation.

TRANSFER: No.

APPEAL: The judgment of the Small Claims Court is conclusive on the plaintiff (that is, he may not appeal although defendant may) except for appeals for wages or labor performed. Appeal must be taken in 5 days by giving notice and payment of $1.50. Appeal is taken to County Court. Denver Court: City and County, Civil Division, 1100 Bannoch, 297-5161.

CONNECTICUT

TYPE: Small Claims.

CLAIM LIMIT: $750.

MINIMUM AGE: 18.

STATUTE OF LIMITATIONS: 2–4 years.

FILING FEES: $3 plus $5 for sheriff's service.

NORMAL WAITING TIME: Varies but generally less than one month throughout the state.

VENUE: District where the plaintiff or where the defendant resides.

ARBITRATION SYSTEM: No.

LAWYERS: May appear for any party but not required.

CORPORATIONS: May appear as plaintiff or defendant. Attorney permitted but not required.

TRANSFER: None.

APPEAL: No appeal from Small Claims Court. (Connecticut Statutes 51–265)

COMMENT: Small Claims Court is a special session of the Circuit Court. The winning party is reimbursed for cash disbursements for entry, mailing, witness and officer fees. In addition, further costs, not exceeding $25, may be awarded by special order of the Court against any party who has sought in any way to hamper a party or court in securing a speedy determination of the case. New Haven Court: 169 Church St., 777-7231.

DELAWARE

TYPE: Justice of the Peace.

CLAIM LIMIT: Less than $1500 in Courts of Justice of the Peace.

MINIMUM AGE: 19.

STATUTE OF LIMITATIONS: 2–4 years.

FILING FEES: $10.

NORMAL WAITING TIME: 3 weeks.

SERVICE OF PROCESS: Constable.

VENUE: Anywhere in state.

ARBITRATION SYSTEM: No.

LAWYERS: May appear but not necessary.

CORPORATIONS: May be plaintiff or defendant and may appear with or without attorney.

TRANSFER: None.

APPEAL: Appeal to Superior Court within 15 days. Defendant must offer security for judgment. Plaintiff may appeal without security if no counterclaim and costs paid. Wilmington Courts: (#10): 2415 Milltown Rd., 999-8502; (#13): 913 King St., 656-1323; (#15): 1601 Concord Pike—Independence Mall, 656-3542.

DISTRICT OF COLUMBIA

TYPE: Small Claims.

CLAIM LIMIT: $750.

MINIMUM AGE: 21.

STATUTE OF LIMITATIONS: 1–4 years.

FILING FEES: $1 plus $0.52 certified mail or $1.50 for marshal's service.

NORMAL WAITING TIME: 2 weeks.

SERVICE OF PROCESS: Certified mail or marshal's service.

VENUE: Small Claims branch of Superior Court handles all of the district.

ARBITRATION SYSTEM: Claims may be arbitrated if parties agree to do so.

LAWYERS: May appear but not required.

CORPORATIONS: May appear as plaintiff or defendant with or without attorney.

TRANSFER: Landlord Tenant cases may be removed to the United States District Court. Other civil cases may be removed to Superior Court at the Court's discretion. If defendant is entitled to a jury trial and so requests, the case is transferred to the regular civil session.

APPEAL: The clerk is required to assist a party in preparing application for allowance of appeal to the District of Columbia Court of Appeals. Application for appeal goes to a panel of three judges and is allowed if any one of the three so orders. Application must be made within three days of judgment.

COMMENTS: The Small Claims and Conciliation Branch is a branch of the Civil Division of the Supreme Court. Address: 613 G St. N.W. (South Potomac Bldg.), 629-4886.

FLORIDA

TYPE: Small Claims.

CLAIM LIMIT: $1500.

MINIMUM AGE: 18.

STATUTE OF LIMITATIONS: 1–4 years.

FILING FEES: Vary with amount of money being sued for: $1–99 : $3.50, $100–999 : $10.00, $999–1500 : $15.00. Fees include price of registered mail service.

NORMAL WAITING TIME: Less than one month.

VENUE: District where defendant lives.

ARBITRATION SYSTEM: None.

LAWYERS: May appear for any party but not required.

CORPORATIONS: May appear as plaintiff or defendant. Lawyer not required.

TRANSFER: Yes, upon motion, but very rare.

APPEAL: Yes.

GEORGIA

TYPE: Small Claims—Justice of the Peace—varying throughout the state.

CLAIM LIMIT: Varies throughout the state ($100 in Atlanta).

MINIMUM AGE: 18.

STATUTE OF LIMITATIONS: 1–4 years.

FILING FEES: Atlanta: $6.50 plus $3.00 for additional defendants, Pauper's affidavit may be substituted by those unable to pay. Fees vary within state.

NORMAL WAITING TIME: 30 to 60 days.

SERVICE OF PROCESS: Marshal's service.

VENUE: Judicial district in which defendant resides.

ARBITRATION SYSTEM: None.

LAWYERS: May appear but not required.

CORPORATIONS: Seems to vary within state with corporations barred as plaintiff in Atlanta.

APPEAL: In Atlanta appeal to appellate division but difficult procedure.

COMMENTS: Small Claims Courts are set up by the counties so limits and practices vary widely and may not exist at all in some areas. In addition to Small Claims Courts, many counties have "short process backs" available that allow persons to use form pleadings and appear in the County Civil Courts without an attorney. The jurisdictional limits for "short process backs" are higher than for "Small Claims Courts." Atlanta Court: Fulton County Courthouse, 160 Pryor St., 572-2101.

HAWAII

TYPE: Small Claims.

CLAIM LIMIT: $300.

MINIMUM AGE: 21.

STATUTE OF LIMITATIONS: 2–6 years.

FILING FEES: $3 plus $4 for service plus mileage. Filing and service fees may be waived on sworn statement of inability to pay.

NORMAL WAITING TIME: 15 days.

SERVICE OF PROCESS: Mail or personal by deputy sheriff.

VENUE: Where cause of action arose or defendant located.

ARBITRATION SYSTEM: None.

LAWYERS: May appear but not required.

CORPORATIONS: May appear as plaintiff or defendant but no attorney required. Court clerks are available to assist private citizens but not corporations.

TRANSFER: Case remains in Small Claims Court even if counterclaim over the limit but can be transferred if a jury trial requested.

APPEAL: No appeal.

COMMENTS: Hawaii Statutes require the publication of a handbook to explain the Small Claims Court to mailmen. This should be available from the Office of the Administration Director of Courts, Judiciary Building, Honolulu, Hawaii 96813. Honolulu Court: 842 Bethal St., 548-2449.

IDAHO

TYPE: Small Claims.

CLAIM LIMIT: Up to $200.

MINIMUM AGE: 21.

STATUTE OF LIMITATIONS: 2–4 years.

FILING FEES: $5 plus service.

NORMAL WAITING TIME: Hearing date set at discretion of judge.

SERVICE OF PROCESS: Personal service or mail service on request.

VENUE: County where one of the defendants resides.

ARBITRATION SYSTEM: No.

LAWYERS: May not appear.

CORPORATIONS: May appear as plaintiff or defendant but attorneys barred for all parties in Small Claims Court.

TRANSFER: No provision.

APPEAL: Appeal must be taken within 30 days and bond posted. Loser must pay $25 attorney's fee to opposing party.

COMMENTS: Small Claims Court is a Department of the Magistrate's Court.

ILLINOIS

TYPE: Small Claims.

CLAIM LIMIT: Less than $1000.

MINIMUM AGE: 18.

STATUTE OF LIMITATIONS: 1–5 years.

FILING FEES: Less than $500: $7; more than $500: $10 plus $1.50 fee for mail service.

NORMAL WAITING TIME: 28 to 40 days. Around 2 weeks in Chicago.

SERVICE OF PROCESS: Certified Mail Service.

VENUE: County where cause of action arose or where one defendant resides.

ARBITRATION SYSTEM: None.

LAWYERS: Attorneys may appear but required only for corporations.

CORPORATIONS: Corporations may appear as plaintiff or defendant but must be represented by attorney.

TRANSFER: No provision.

APPEAL: Must be taken within 30 days and within 5 days for rent actions. Same appeal provision for Small Claims as for regular session of the Municipal Court.

COMMENTS: Defendant may make demand for jury. Cost of jury trial is $25 for 12 person jury and $12.50 for 6 person jury. This right is rarely used. Installment payment of judgments may not be extended over a period exceeding three years. Chicago Court: Rm 601, Chicago Civic Center, Washington St., 321-8100.

INDIANA

TYPE: Justice of the Peace.

CLAIM LIMIT: Justice of the Peace courts less than $500.

MINIMUM AGE: 21.

STATUTE OF LIMITATIONS: 2–6 years.

FILING FEES: $6.

NORMAL WAITING TIME: Two weeks.

SERVICE OF PROCESS: Constable.

VENUE: One defendant must live in county.

ARBITRATION SYSTEM: No.

LAWYERS: May appear but required only for corporations.

CORPORATIONS: May appear as plaintiff or defendant but must be represented by an attorney.

TRANSFER: Indiana Statutes 5–403 provide for transfer to Municipal or City Court on affidavit of inability to get a fair trial in Justice of the Peace Court.

APPEAL: To Circuit or Superior Court for trial de novo. Appeal must be taken in 30 days although this time is extendable if appellant can show he/she was prevented by circumstances beyond control. Appeal bond must be posted.

COMMENTS: January 1, 1972, the constitutional provision requiring Justice of the Peace Courts in each county was deleted so Justice of the Peace Courts have now been abolished in some counties. Wayne Township Justices: Allen County Courthouses, 715 S. Calhoun St., 423-7327, 423-7177.

IOWA

TYPE: Justice of the Peace—Conciliation Court.

CLAIM LIMIT: Justice of the Peace Courts: Less than $100. If parties consent up to $300. Conciliation Court Sessions must be utilized in district court sessions for claims less than $100.

MINIMUM AGE: 19.

STATUTE OF LIMITATIONS: 2–5 years.

FILING FEES: $1 plus seven cents per mile for constable service in Justice of the Peace Courts.

SERVICE OF PROCESS: Constable or sheriff.

VENUE: Where cause of action occurred or defendant resides.

ARBITRATION SYSTEM: In District Court conciliation session.

LAWYERS: Not allowed in Conciliation Court but allowed in Justice of the Peace Court.

CORPORATIONS: May appear as plaintiff or defendant but may not bring attorney to conciliation court.

TRANSFER: No.

APPEAL: After June 1, 1973, review of conciliation decision is discretionary. Petition for review must be made within 10 days. Justice of the Peace decision may be appealed to Superior Court.

COMMENTS: District, Municipal and Superior courts are all empowered to set up conciliation sessions. These are informal sessions with no record and no counsel allowed. Parties may not proceed on a claim less than $100 unless first a good faith effort at conciliation has been made.

KANSAS

TYPE: Small Claims.

CLAIM LIMIT: Less than $100 in Small Claims division of City Court.

MINIMUM AGE: 18.

STATUTE OF LIMITATIONS: 1–4 years.

FILING FEES: $10 deposit for costs.

NORMAL WAITING TIME: A few weeks.

SERVICE OF PROCESS: Marshal or constable.

VENUE: County where defendant resides or where plaintiff resides if the defendant is located there or where the cause of action arose or where the defendant has a place of employment or business and is served there.

ARBITRATION SYSTEM: Must have prior conciliation court hearing without attorneys.

LAWYERS: Not allowed at conciliation hearing.

CORPORATIONS: May appear as plaintiff or defendant and may be represented by an attorney except at the conciliation hearing. Clerk's help in preparation is available to individual parties but not to corporations.

TRANSFER: No provision.

APPEAL: May appeal to district court if more than $50.

COMMENTS: Kansas Statutes 20–1301 provided for a small debtor's court for claims less than $20. This has been replaced by the city courts established by 20–1618 and 20–2419–2436.

KENTUCKY

TYPE: Justice of the Peace.

CLAIM LIMIT: Justice of the Peace Courts have exclusive jurisdiction of claims less than $50 and concurrent jurisdiction of claims of $50 to $500.

MINIMUM AGE: 18.

STATUTE OF LIMITATIONS: 1–5 years.

FILING FEES: $1 to $6.50 depending on size of claim and location.

NORMAL WAITING TIME: 30 days after service.

SERVICE OF PROCESS: By constable or sheriff.

VENUE: County in which plaintiff or defendant resides or where defendant can be summoned.

ARBITRATION SYSTEM: No provision.

LAWYERS: May appear but not required.

CORPORATIONS: May appear as plaintiffs or defendants. No statutory provisions barring attorneys.

TRANSFER: No provision.

APPEAL: New trial available in quarterly court. Certified copy of judgment and amount of costs must be filed in court to which appeal taken.

COMMENTS: Louisville Court: 589-3060.

LOUISIANA

TYPE: New Orleans, City Court; elsewhere, Justice of the Peace.

CLAIM LIMIT: Outside New Orleans, Justice of the Peace Courts are limited to less than $100 and city courts to less than $500. In New Orleans the city court has exclusive original jurisdiction of claims less than $100 and concurrent on claims from $100 to $5000.

MINIMUM AGE: 21.

STATUTE OF LIMITATIONS: One year.

FILING FEES: $10 in Justice of the Peace.

NORMAL WAITING TIME: Two weeks to one month.

SERVICE OF PROCESS: Constable.

VENUE: In Parish of domicile of defendant.

ARBITRATION SYSTEM: No provision.

LAWYERS: May appear but not required.

CORPORATIONS: May appear as plaintiff or defendant, with or without attorney.

TRANSFER: No provision.

APPEAL: Appeal may be taken if a question of law. In the First City Court of the City of New Orleans, claims less than $100 are taken to the civil district court of the Parish of Orleans and all others are taken to the State Court of Appeals for the Fourth Circuit. Bond must be posted.

COMMENTS: City Courts, Justice of the Peace Courts, and District Courts are not courts of record. Revised Statutes 13:1872 replaced Justice of the Peace Courts with city judges in cities greater than 5000. New Orleans Court: Room 201, Civil Courts Building, 421 Loyola Ave., 523-2220, 523-1775.

MAINE

TYPE: Small Claims.

CLAIM LIMIT: $200.

MINIMUM AGE: 20.

STATUTE OF LIMITATIONS: 2–6 years.

FILING FEES: $5.

NORMAL WAITING TIME: Portland, about one month.

SERVICE OF PROCESS: Ordinary mail service.

VENUE: Judicial district in which plaintiff or defendant resides.

ARBITRATION SYSTEM: No provision.

LAWYERS: May appear but not required.

CORPORATIONS: May appear as plaintiff or defendant with or without lawyer.

TRANSFER: No provision.

APPEAL: Points of law may be appealed to Superior Court.

COMMENTS: Small Claims are heard by judges of the district courts. Portland Court: Cumberland County Court House, 142 Federal Street, 772-3715.

MARYLAND

TYPE: Small Claims.

CLAIM LIMIT: $1000 for claims without formal pleadings.

MINIMUM AGE: 21 except with guardian or "next friend," e.g. an adult.

STATUTE OF LIMITATIONS: 1–4 years.

FILING FEES: $5 for claims up to $500; $10 for larger claims.

NORMAL WAITING TIME: 30 days.

SERVICE OF PROCESS: Constables or sheriffs.

VENUE: In county where defendant resides or is employed habitually or does business.

ARBITRATION SYSTEM: No provision.

LAWYERS: May appear but not required.

CORPORATIONS: May appear as plaintiff or defendant and may be represented by an attorney.

TRANSFER: No provision.

APPEAL: Appeal may be made within 30 days. On claims less than $500 trial is de novo. On claims from district court of $500 to $2500, appeal may be de novo or on the record only.

COMMENTS: The court system in Maryland was revamped in 1972. The District Courts of General Jurisdiction now have jurisdiction of claims less than $5000 and exclusive jurisdiction of claims less than $2500. On claims less than $1000 no formal pleadings are required. On claims greater than $500 there is a right to claim trial by jury.

MASSACHUSETTS

TYPE: Small Claims.

CLAIM LIMIT: Less than $400 on claim plus double or treble damages for statutory penalties.

MINIMUM AGE: 21.

STATUTE OF LIMITATIONS: 2–6 years.

FILING FEES: $3 entry fee is statutory maximum. Lower fees and registered mail costs are in discretion of court. Boston is $1.25 entry and $0.53 charge for registered mail. In Cambridge the total cost is $2.26.

NORMAL WAITING TIME: 2 to 8 weeks. In Boston 4 to 6.

SERVICE OF PROCESS: Registered mail or constable may be used.

VENUE: In judicial district where defendant lives or has usual place of business.

ARBITRATION SYSTEM: No provision.

LAWYERS: May appear but not required.

CORPORATIONS: May appear as plaintiff or defendant with or without attorney.

TRANSFER: Case may be removed to Superior Court on payment of $5 fee and posting of $100 bond. Case may then, however, be remanded to a district court and normally is.

APPEAL: No appeal from Small Claims Court. The only possibility is to preserve removal to Superior Court by removing from Small Claims Court initially. Then, upon payment of another $5 fee it may be removed to Superior Court again.

COMMENTS: There is currently an appreciable amount of petition circulating and other lobbying for Small Claims Court reform in Massachusetts. Evening and Saturday sessions, etc., would help; but the main problems are the specific one of inadequate collection mechanism and the general one of a court system characterized by political appointments. A new Small Claims Court bill is reportedly being drafted by the Attorney General. Selected Courts: *Boston*: Boston Municipal Court, Rm.

374, Old Court House, 742-9250-Ext. 545; *Brighton*: Brighton District Court, 54 Academy Hill Road, 782-6521; *Cambridge*: Eastern Middlesex County Third District Court, Third St., 876-8000; *Fall River*: Briston County Second District Court, Main Street, 678-4511; *Holyoke*: Police Department Building, High Street, 534-5019; *New Bedford*: 505 Pleasant St., 997-4503; *Worcester*: 50 Harvard St., 756-2441.

MICHIGAN

TYPE: Small Claims.

CLAIM LIMIT: Less than $300 with $500 exception in some cities.

MINIMUM AGE: 21.

STATUTE OF LIMITATIONS: 2–10 years.

FILING FEES: $5 plus $2 per defendant. Detroit: $8 plus $4 per defendant.

NORMAL WAITING TIME: One month up to three months in Detroit.

SERVICE OF PROCESS: Court officer or a disinterested person the judge may designate.

VENUE: County where defendant is established.

ARBITRATION SYSTEM: No provision.

LAWYERS: May appear but not required.

CORPORATIONS: May appear as plaintiff or defendant with or without an attorney.

TRANSFER: Defendant may demand transfer to regular session of the district court.

APPEAL: May appeal to Circuit Court but there is a presumption of validity of the lower court judge's determination of the evidence.

COMMENTS: Small Claims is a division of the district court. Ann Arbor Court: City Hall—6th floor, 100 N. Fifth Ave., 761-2400 Ext. 211; Detroit: Room 1101, City-County Building, 2 Woodward Ave., 224-5456.

MINNESOTA

TYPE: Conciliation Court.

CLAIM LIMIT: Minnesota statutes provide that a city or village may establish a Conciliation Court with jurisdiction under $300. Exceptions are made for Ramsey County (Saint Paul), Hennepin County (Minneapolis), and Duluth where jurisdiction goes up to $500.

MINIMUM AGE: 21.

STATUTE OF LIMITATIONS: 2–6 years.

FILING FEES: Statute limits to $3 for filing and serving.

NORMAL WAITING TIME: 6 to 8 weeks.

SERVICE OF PROCESS: Plaintiff may serve.

VENUE: Where defendant lives unless defendant is not a resident and then where plaintiff resides.

ARBITRATION SYSTEM: Yes.

LAWYERS: No attorneys allowed.

CORPORATIONS: May appear as plaintiff or defendant.

TRANSFER: May be removed to Municipal Court through an attorney.

APPEAL: Within 10 days after entry of judgment by filing bond and affidavit removing and $5. Appeal is then tried in the Municipal Court. There is no appeal from the Municipal Court on removal from Conciliation Court.

COMMENTS: Minneapolis Court: 441 Court House, 330-2602; St. Paul Court: Conciliation Court, 1200 City and County Courthouse, 15 West Kellogg St., 223-4317.

MISSISSIPPI

TYPE: Justice of the Peace.

CLAIM LIMIT: Less than $200 in Justice of the Peace Courts.

MINIMUM AGE: None.

STATUTE OF LIMITATIONS: 1–6 years.

FILING FEES: $6 including service.

NORMAL WAITING TIME: Varies according to the schedule of the local Justice of the Peace.

SERVICE OF PROCESS: Constable or sheriff or someone else appointed by Justice of the Peace.

VENUE: Judicial district in which cause of action arose or defendant resides.

ARBITRATION SYSTEM: No provision.

LAWYERS: May appear but not required.

CORPORATIONS: May appear as plaintiff or defendant with or without attorney.

TRANSFER: No provision.

APPEAL: Either party may appeal within 10 days. A bond for double the amount with a minimum of $100 in controversy must be posted. A new trial is held on appeal.

COMMENTS: Mississippi has a Justice of the Peace system with few statutory controls so practice varies widely according to the individual Justice. On or before the return day of the process, either party may demand a trial by jury of six.

MISSOURI

TYPE: Magistrate's Court.

CLAIM LIMIT: Jurisdictional limit of Magistrate's Court varies from $2000 to $3500 depending on the population of the county.

MINIMUM AGE: 21.

STATUTE OF LIMITATIONS: 2–5 years.

FILING FEES: $9.

NORMAL WAITING TIME: 3 to 4 weeks.

SERVICE OF PROCESS: Constable service at last and usual place of abode.

VENUE: Where defendant resides or where plaintiff resides and defendant may be found or in actions for damage where the cause of action occurred.

ARBITRATION SYSTEM: No provision.

LAWYERS: May appear but not required.

CORPORATIONS: May appear as plaintiff or defendant with or without attorney.

TRANSFER: No provision.

APPEAL: New trial in Circuit Court.

COMMENTS: Justice of the Peace Courts business was taken over by Magistrate's Courts in a statutory revision. Kansas City Court: Jackson County Court House, 7th floor, 415 E. 12th St., 221-8500.

MONTANA

TYPE: Justice's Court.

CLAIM LIMIT: Less than $300.

MINIMUM AGE: 19.

STATUTE OF LIMITATIONS: 2–4 years.

FILING FEES: $2.50 (Provision to Pauper's affidavit in lieu of costs).

NORMAL WAITING TIME: Date set by parties.

SERVICE OF PROCESS: Sheriff or constable or male resident of state more than 18.

VENUE: Judicial district where defendant lives or may be served personally.

ARBITRATION SYSTEM: None.

LAWYERS: Attorneys may appear but not required.

CORPORATIONS: May appear as plaintiff or defendant with or without attorney.

TRANSFER: May be transferred within 7 days of service.

APPEAL: May be appealed to district court within 30 days for a new trial. Bond, twice the amount in controversy, must be posted or deposit made in amount of the judgment plus $300.

COMMENTS: There is a right to jury trial in the Justice's Courts. If a defendant offers settlement before trial and plaintiff refuses, plaintiff loses the award of costs. Defendant must file a written answer to complaint. Ordinary Court rules apply in theory, but atmosphere usually informal.

NEBRASKA

TYPE: Metropolitan, Small Claims; rural, Justice of the Peace.

CLAIM LIMIT: Justice of the Peace: $200. Small Claims Division of Municipal Courts: $500.

MINIMUM AGE: 19.

STATUTE OF LIMITATIONS: 1–4 years.

FILING FEES: $4 for Municipal Court.

NORMAL WAITING TIME: A few weeks.

SERVICE OF PROCESS: Mail in Small Claims Court. Personal service in Justice of the Peace Court.

VENUE: Where cause of action arose or defendant resides.

ARBITRATION SYSTEM: No provision.

LAWYERS: No attorneys in Small Claims Court.

CORPORATIONS: Corporations may appear as defendants and may appear as plaintiffs but are limited to 10 affirmative suits a year in Small Claims Court.

TRANSFER: Small Claims are transferred to the Municipal Courts if either side retains an attorney.

APPEAL: Appeal may be taken from the Justice of the Peace Court to District Court by filing notice of appeal within 10 days. An undertaking of twice the amount of the judgment must be made. Appeal of Small Claims Court is to the regular session of the Municipal Court.

COMMENTS: Justice of the Peace Courts exist outside urban areas. Municipal Courts replace them in metropolitan areas. The Small Claims division of Municipal Courts started operating January, 1973. Nebraska Statutes 25–1801 is a general statutory provision which provides that on any claim for less than $200 if demand by the plaintiff is made 90 days prior to institution of a suit and no payment is made, plaintiff is entitled to recover costs, 6% interest from date of presentation of claim, and attorney's costs if he secures judgment in his favor. Jury may be demanded in Justice Court. $3 per juror is taxed as part of costs against the losing party. Omaha Court: 341-8122.

NEVADA

TYPE: Small Claims.

CLAIM LIMIT: $300.

MINIMUM AGE: 18 females; 21 males.

STATUTE OF LIMITATIONS: 2–3 years.

FILING FEES: $5 filing fee.

NORMAL WAITING TIME: 5 to 15 days from issuance of order.

SERVICE OF PROCESS: Mail or personal.

VENUE: In township or city where defendant resides unless there is no Justices Council in the township or city—then any part of same county.

ARBITRATION SYSTEM: None.

LAWYERS: May appear but not required.

CORPORATIONS: May appear as plaintiff or defendant with or without attorney.

TRANSFER: No provision.

APPEAL: May appeal within 5 days to District Court on posting bond in amount of judgment plus $15 attorney's fees.

COMMENTS: Small Claims Court is a part of the Justice's Court system.

NEW HAMPSHIRE

TYPE: Small Claims.

CLAIM LIMIT: Less than $300.

MINIMUM AGE: 21.

STATUTE OF LIMITATIONS: 2–6 years.

FILING FEES: $1.50 entry fee plus postage.

NORMAL WAITING TIME: Less than one month.

SERVICE OF PROCESS: Post paid registered mail.

VENUE: Municipal Court of town or city where plaintiff or defendant resides. If no Municipal Court in the town or city, any town or city in the county.

ARBITRATION SYSTEM: No provision.

LAWYERS: May appear but not required.

CORPORATIONS: May appear as plaintiff or defendants with or without attorney.

TRANSFER: No provision.

APPEAL: Only on questions of law to New Hampshire Supreme Court.

COMMENTS: Small Claims are heard before Municipal Court justices. Small Claims is an alternative simplified procedure.

NEW JERSEY

TYPE: Small Claims.

CLAIM LIMIT: Less than $200 except for security deposit claims up to $50.

MINIMUM AGE: 21.

STATUTE OF LIMITATIONS: 2–6 years.

FILING FEES: New Jersey Statute 2A–18–65 provides for 2/10 summons fee plus 40¢ for each additional defendant plus 10¢ per mile for constable service.

NORMAL WAITING TIME: Less than one month.

SERVICE OF PROCESS: Mail or constable.

VENUE: County where defendant resides.

ARBITRATION SYSTEM: No provision.

LAWYERS: May appear but not required.

CORPORATIONS: May appear as plaintiff or defendant with or without an attorney.

TRANSFER: Upon counterclaim greater than $200.

APPEAL: Under same procedure as all appeals from County District Court to Appellate Division of the Superior Court.

COMMENTS: County District Court Judge sits in special session for Small Claims. Elizabeth Court: 351-5000; Newark: Old Court House, 470 High St., 961-7204; 961-7196; Trenton: County Court House, Broad St., 989-8000.

NEW MEXICO

TYPE: Small Claims.

CLAIM LIMIT: Small Claims Court established in counties with population greater than 100,000 may hear claims up to $2000.

MINIMUM AGE: 18.

STATUTE OF LIMITATIONS: 3–4 years.

FILING FEES: $6.50 and service.

NORMAL WAITING TIME: Varies by location.

SERVICE OF PROCESS: Personal by sheriff or marshal.

VENUE: Where cause of action arose or defendant resides.

ARBITRATION SYSTEM: No provision.

LAWYERS: May appear but not required.

CORPORATIONS: May appear as plaintiff or defendant with or without attorney.

TRANSFER: May transfer to District Court by claiming jury trial and paying jury fee.

APPEAL: May appeal to District Court within 30 days by posting appeal bond with two or more sureties. No new evidence is allowed on appeal and findings of fact of the Small Claims Court are binding. Appeal is taken only on questions of law.

NEW YORK

TYPE: Small Claims.

CLAIM LIMIT: $500.

MINIMUM AGE: 21.

STATUTE OF LIMITATIONS: 1–6 years.

FILING FEES: $2 plus charge for registered mail service which varies between $1 and $2.

NORMAL WAITING TIME: From 2 weeks in Queens (New York Civil Court, Borough of Queens) up. Manhattan around one month. Brooklyn 2-7 weeks.

SERVICE OF PROCESS: Registered mail.

VENUE: In general, the county where one defendant resides. The New York City Civil Court's Small Claims Division may be used for defendants who have an office or employment in the City as well as City residents.

ARBITRATION SYSTEM: There is a voluntary arbitration proceeding available in some parts of the State with a shorter waiting time than waiting for trial with judge.

LAWYERS: Corporations must appear through an attorney. For other parties, lawyers may appear but are not required.

CORPORATIONS: No corporation nor assignee of claim may appear as plaintiff. Corporations must appear as defendant through an attorney.

TRANSFER: The court has the power to transfer a case from the Small Claims docket to another part of the court. A case is transferred if a counterclaim of over $500 is filed and the defendant pays the ceiling fee as if presented in that court.

APPEAL: The right of appeal is waived unless "substantial injustice" can be shown.

COMMENTS: The New York City Civil Court, Small Claims Division may be used for defendants who live in, have an office in, or regular employment in New York City. There are also Small Claims divisions of the District and County Courts. Defendants may file demand for jury trial if accompanied by affidavit that there are issues of fact requiring such a trial and an undertaking of $50 for costs. The New York City Court is a good one. Selected Courts: *Albany*: City Hall, Eagle St., 472-5173; *Bronx*: 851 Gran Concourse, 293-6500; *Brooklyn*: 120 Schermerhorn St., 643-8180; *Manhattan*: 111 Centre St., 566-3824; *Queens*: 126-06 Queens Blvd., Kew Gardens, 544-9300; *Rochester*: Hall of Justice, Room 1, Exchange St., 232-7070; *Staten Island (Richmond)*: 927 Castelton Ave., 442-8000; *White Plains*: Small Claims Part, City Court, 279 Hamilton Ave., 949-4800 Ext. 296.

NORTH CAROLINA

TYPE: Small Claims.

CLAIM LIMIT: Magistrate's Court has jurisdiction of matters involving less than $300.

MINIMUM AGE: 18.

STATUTE OF LIMITATIONS: 6 months–4 years.

FILING FEES: Less than $100: $7; $100-$300: $10; plus $2 for each additional defendant to be served.

NORMAL WAITING TIME: Around one month.

SERVICE OF PROCESS: Sheriff serves.

VENUE: Where cause of action arose or where defendant resides.

ARBITRATION SYSTEM: None.

LAWYERS: May appear with or without.

CORPORATIONS: May appear as plaintiff or defendant with or without lawyer.

TRANSFER: To Superior Court in 5 days if requested by defendant.

APPEAL: May get trial de novo in District Court in 10 days. Serve written notice on all parties or may ask orally in open court. Jury trial may be demanded on appeal. Execution is stayed if undertaking filed with one or more sureties.

COMMENTS: Small Claims actions are filed with the clerk of the Superior Court and tried before a magistrate.

NORTH DAKOTA

TYPE: Small Claims.

CLAIM LIMIT: Less than $200.

MINIMUM AGE: 18.

STATUTE OF LIMITATIONS: 2–6 years.

FILING FEES: $2 for filing plus $1 per defendant.

NORMAL WAITING TIME: 5 to 30 days after service or receipt by defendant.

SERVICE OF PROCESS: Certified mail or personal.

VENUE: County of defendant's residence.

ARBITRATION SYSTEM: None.

LAWYERS: May appear but not required.

CORPORATIONS: May appear as plaintiff or defendant with or without attorney.

TRANSFER: No provision.

APPEAL: Appeal must be taken within 10 days. Appeal is to the District Court of the County. Notice of the appeal and a copy of the bond required by the District Court clerk must be filed with the opposing party within five days after appeal is taken.

COMMENTS: The Small Claims Court is a division of the County Court. A jury of six may be demanded.

OHIO

TYPE: Small Claims.

CLAIM LIMIT: Less than $150.

MINIMUM AGE: 21.

STATUTE OF LIMITATIONS: 1–4 years.

FILING FEES: $2 plus 75¢ for certified mail.

NORMAL WAITING TIME: Less than one month.

SERVICE OF PROCESS: Mail or personal.

VENUE: County where defendant resides or cause of action arose.

ARBITRATION SYSTEM: State statute allows voluntary conciliation proceeding.

LAWYERS: May appear but not required.

CORPORATIONS: May appear as plaintiff or defendant with or without attorney but corporations may not "engage in cross examination, argument or other acts of an advocacy" without an attorney.

TRANSFER: Transfer to regular docket of Municipal or Civil Court allowed on defendant's motion before trial.

APPEAL: No appeal. Failure to file for jury trial waives appeal.

COMMENTS: Small Claims is division of Municipal or City Court. Selected Courts: *Akron*: Room 837, Safety Bldg., 217 High St., 375-2922; *Cincinnati*: Room 123a, Hamilton County Court House, Court and Main Sts., 632-8315; *Columbus*: Room 217, Safety Bldg., Gay St., 461-7381; *Dayton*: Basement—Price Bldg., 367 W. 2nd St., 225-5363; *Youngstown*: City Hall, Boardman and Phelps, 744-4181 Ext. 209.

OKLAHOMA

TYPE: Small Claims.

CLAIM LIMIT: Less than $400.

MINIMUM AGE: Male 21; Female 18.

STATUTE OF LIMITATIONS: 1–5 years.

FILING FEES: $3; $10 in actions for possesion of personal property.

NORMAL WAITING TIME: Less than 4 weeks.

SERVICE OF PROCESS: Certified mail.

VENUE: Where cause of action arose.

ARBITRATION SYSTEM: No provision.

LAWYERS: May appear but not required.

CORPORATIONS: May appear as plaintiff or defendant with or without lawyer. Collection agency, collection agent, or assignee of claim may not appear.

TRANSFER: Defendant may move for transfer to another docket of the District Court. Defendant must then deposit $25 as the court cost.

APPEAL: Appeals must be taken to the Supreme Court. Must file petition in review within 30 days and post bond for judgment and costs.

COMMENTS: Defendant's counterclaim or set off must be filed and served on plaintiff at least 48 hours prior to trial date. Either party may request a reporter or jury 48 hours before the hearing and deposit $25.

OREGON

TYPE: Small Claims.

CLAIM LIMIT: Less than $20 exclusive jurisdiction in Small Claims department of District Court. $20 to $500 in concurrent jurisdiction with District Court.

MINIMUM AGE: 21.

STATUTE OF LIMITATIONS: 2–6 years.

FILING FEES: Less than $20: $1; $20–$100: $2; $100–$200: $3; $200–$300: $4; $300–$400: $5; $400–$500: $6. Defendant must pay $1 fee.

NORMAL WAITING TIME: Two weeks.

SERVICE OF PROCESS: Sheriff, deputy, constable or other competent person over 21 who is an Oregon resident and not an attorney.

VENUE: Where defendant resides or may be found.

ARBITRATION SYSTEM: No provision.

LAWYERS: May appear only with consent of judge.

CORPORATIONS: May appear as plaintiff or defendant but lawyer may act only as to removal.

TRANSFER: May be had to next highest court if more than $20 involved.

APPEAL: The judgment of the Small Claims Court is final upon the plaintiff. The defendant may appeal to the Circuit Court within 10 days after entry of judgment. If defendant loses on appeal, he/she must pay $10 to plaintiff as an attorney's fee.

COMMENTS: Oregon Statutes 55.011 created the Small Claims division of the Justice Courts. Claims less than $20 must be heard in Small Claims. Claims of $20 to $500 may be heard in Small Claims or under regular Justice Court proceedings. There is a constitutional right to jury trial in Oregon on claims greater than $20. If jury trial demanded, plaintiff must file formal pleadings.

PENNSYLVANIA

TYPE: Metropolitan, Small Claims; rural, Justice of the Peace.

CLAIM LIMIT: Outside Philadelphia Justice of the Peace Courts hear claims of less than $500.

MINIMUM AGE: Minor may appear in Justice of the Peace without a guardian. (Rule 802).

STATUTE OF LIMITATIONS: 1–6 years.

FILING FEES: Philadelphia Municipal Court: $6 for certified mail. $6 for personal service.

NORMAL WAITING TIME: Varies widely across the state. About 2 months in Philadelphia.

SERVICE OF PROCESS: In Justice of the Peace Court or Municipal Court, plaintiff may choose mail (Rule 566). If mail not requested, service by constable or sheriff.

VENUE: Where defendant may be served or where transaction took place.

ARBITRATION SYSTEM: No provision.

LAWYERS: May appear but not required.

CORPORATIONS: May appear as plaintiff or defendant. Attorney required in Philadelphia.

TRANSFER: No provision.

APPEAL: Justice of the Peace: New trial in Court of Common Pleas, which may deny further appeal. Appeal must be taken in 20 days. No bond or other security is required. Philadelphia Municipal Court: Appeal within 30 days to Court of Common Pleas.

COMMENTS: Philadelphia Court: Rooms 195–196, City Hall, Broad and Market Sts., 686-7987.

PUERTO RICO

TYPE: Small Claims.

CLAIM LIMIT: Less than $2500 in District Court; Small Claims less than $100.

MINIMUM AGE: 21.

STATUTE OF LIMITATIONS: 1–5 years.

FILING FEES: $1.

NORMAL WAITING TIME: Date may be set by plaintiff 5 days after service of defendant.

SERVICE OF PROCESS: Mail, telegraph, or any other written communication.

VENUE: Where cause of action arose.

ARBITRATION SYSTEM: No provision.

LAWYERS: May appear but not required.

CORPORATIONS: May appear as plaintiff or defendant with or without attorney.

TRANSFER: No provision.

APPEAL: May appeal to District Court.

RHODE ISLAND

TYPE: Small Claims.

CLAIM LIMIT: Less than $300.

MINIMUM AGE: 21.

STATUTE OF LIMITATIONS: 1–6 years.

FILING FEES: $1, plus $0.60 mail service.

NORMAL WAITING TIME: 4 to 6 weeks.

SERVICE OF PROCESS: Mail.

VENUE: District where plaintiff or defendant resides.

ARBITRATION SYSTEM: No provision.

LAWYERS: Allowed and required for corporate plaintiffs.

CORPORATIONS: May appear as Plaintiff or Defendant. Must be represented by attorney if plaintiff.

TRANSFER: By counterclaim in excess of $300.

APPEAL: May be appealed only by defendant on $50 fee and $20 costs.

COMMENTS: Small Claims Court is a division of the District Court System. Providence Court: R.I. District Court, 150 Benefit St., 331-1603.

SOUTH CAROLINA

TYPE: Magistrate's Court.

CLAIM LIMIT: $200 general provision. Varies for particular counties, e.g., Chester county $1000.

MINIMUM AGE: 21.

STATUTE OF LIMITATIONS: 2–6 years.

FILING FEES: Fees vary from county to county. Service $1, plus 50¢ per mile.

NORMAL WAITING TIME: Varies within the State.

SERVICE OF PROCESS: Sheriff.

VENUE: Where cause of action arose or defendant resides.

ARBITRATION SYSTEM: No provision.

LAWYERS: May appear but not required.

CORPORATIONS: May appear as plaintiff or defendant with or without attorney.

TRANSFER: No provision.

APPEAL: Circuit judges may hear appeal from Magistrates and Municipal Courts. Must give notice 10 days in advance.

SOUTH DAKOTA

TYPE: Small Claims.

CLAIM LIMIT: Less than $100 in Justice or Police Courts. Less than $500 in District or Municipal Courts.

MINIMUM AGE: 18.

STATUTE OF LIMITATIONS: 2–6 years.

FILING FEES: $2 entry fee, plus $1.50 for county law library fund assessed some counties.

NORMAL WAITING TIME: Usually no more than two weeks.

SERVICE OF PROCESS: Mail.

VENUE: Where cause of action arose or defendant resides.

ARBITRATION SYSTEM: No provision.

LAWYERS: No restrictions.

CORPORATIONS: May appear as plaintiff or defendant with or without attorney.

TRANSFER: Plaintiff waives trial by jury and right to appeal by commencing in Small Claims. Defendant may remove to Superior Court by paying $5 and posting a bond for costs.

APPEAL: Plaintiff waives right of appeal by bringing in Small Claims Court. Defendant may remove for jury trial, but only the plaintiff may appeal from such a jury trial.

COMMENTS: The Supreme Court of South Dakota is empowered to make rules for a Small Claims procedure to be utilized by Justice, Police Magistrate's, District, County and Municipal Courts. By bringing action under Small Claims procedure, the plaintiff waives right to trial by jury and right to appeal to the Circuit Court unless the action has been removed to the Circuit, County, or Municipal Court.

TENNESSEE

TYPE: Justice of the Peace.

CLAIM LIMIT: Less than $3000.

MINIMUM AGE: 18.

STATUTE OF LIMITATIONS: 1–4 years.

FILING FEES: $25 cash bond or Pauper's oath in Court of General Sessions. Justice of the Peace Courts require security for costs which may be waived for residents.

NORMAL WAITING TIME: Varies throughout the state.

SERVICE OF PROCESS: Sheriff.

VENUE: Where defendant resides or personal injury or property damage occurred.

ARBITRATION SYSTEM: None.

LAWYERS: May appear but not required.

CORPORATIONS: May appear as plaintiff or defendant with or without attorney.

TRANSFER: No provision.

APPEAL: May appeal within 10 days.

COMMENTS: Tennessee Statutes 16–1101 established Courts of General Sessions for some cities to take over Justice of the Peace jurisdiction.

TEXAS

TYPE: Small Claims.

CLAIM LIMIT: Less than $150 except $200 for wages or labor performed.

MINIMUM AGE: 18.

STATUTE OF LIMITATIONS: 1–4 years.

FILING FEES: $3 filing fee; $2 citation fee.

NORMAL WAITING TIME: 5 to 6 weeks.

SERVICE OF PROCESS: Personal by sheriff or constable.

VENUE: County in which defendant resides or cause of action arose.

ARBITRATION SYSTEM: No provision.

LAWYERS: May appear but not required.

CORPORATIONS: Person, firm partnership, or corporation engaged either primarily or secondarily in the business of lending money at interest or collection agency cannot use Small Claims Court.

TRANSFER: No provision.

APPEAL: To County Court. Trial de novo available if claim greater than $20. No further pleadings required and judgment of that court final.

COMMENTS: Jury trial available by paying $3 jury fee one day prior. Small Claims Court for each city with Justices of the Peace sitting as judges.

UTAH

TYPE: Small Claims.

CLAIM LIMIT: $200.

MINIMUM AGE: Male 21; Female 18.

STATUTE OF LIMITATIONS: 1–4 years.

FILING FEES: $3 plus service fee of $1 plus 20¢ per mile.

NORMAL WAITING TIME: 20 days.

SERVICE OF PROCESS: Court directs sheriff or constable to serve.

VENUE: Where defendant resides or cause of action arose.

ARBITRATION SYSTEM: No provision.

LAWYERS: May appear but not required.

CORPORATIONS: May appear as plaintiff or defendant with no lawyer required.

TRANSFER: No provision.

APPEAL: May appeal to District Court, but that decision is final. Must file notice of appeal within one month and make deposit for costs.

COMMENTS: Salt Lake City Court: Room A–222, Municipal Courts Bldg., 240 East 4th St., 328-7791.

VIRGIN ISLANDS

TYPE: Small Claims.
CLAIM LIMIT: Less than $300.
MINIMUM AGE: 21.
STATUTE OF LIMITATIONS: 1–10 years.
FILING FEES: $1 Small Claims filing fee.
NORMAL WAITING TIME: 5 to 15 days.
SERVICE OF PROCESS: Marshal or other person desig-
    nated by the Court.
VENUE: Where defendant resides or is served.
ARBITRATION SYSTEM: There is a conciliation division
    of the Municipal Court and any party may request
    an attempt be made to settle the dispute at an in-
    formal hearing. In Small Claims the judge must
    first make an attempt to resolve informally.
LAWYERS: No lawyers allowed in Small Claims.
CORPORATIONS: May appear as plaintiff or defendant
    through personal representative but not through
    lawyer.
TRANSFER: No provision.
APPEAL: Findings of fact set aside only if clearly
    erroneous.
COMMENTS: Small Claims is a division of the Municipal
    Court with concurrent jurisdiction to the Municipal
    Court. Municipal Courts also have Conciliation
    Courts.

VERMONT

TYPE: Small Claims.

CLAIM LIMIT: $250.

MINIMUM AGE: 18.

STATUTE OF LIMITATIONS: 3–6 years.

FILING FEES: Less than $100: $2 plus 55¢ postage; $100–$150: $5 plus 55¢ postage.

NORMAL WAITING TIME: 1 to 3 weeks.

SERVICE OF PROCESS: Personal or registered mail.

VENUE: Where defendant resides.

ARBITRATION SYSTEM: No provision.

LAWYERS: May appear but not required.

CORPORATIONS: May appear as plaintiff or defendant with or without lawyer.

TRANSFER: No provision.

APPEAL: None.

COMMENTS: Plaintiff waives jury trial by filing in Small Claims. Defendant may have jury trial by paying $4 and filing affidavit of reason needed for trial by jury.

VIRGINIA

TYPE: "Court Not of Record."

CLAIM LIMIT: Courts Not of Record have exclusive jurisdiction. Under $300 and concurrent $300 to $3000.

MINIMUM AGE: Infant must sue with "next friend" but infant not defined.

STATUTE OF LIMITATIONS: 2–5 years.

FILING FEES: $3.25.

NORMAL WAITING TIME: Two weeks.

SERVICE OF PROCESS: Sheriff.

VENUE: Where cause of action arose or defendant resides.

ARBITRATION SYSTEM: No provision.

LAWYERS: May appear but not required.

CORPORATIONS: May appear as plaintiff or defendant with or without attorney.

TRANSFER: Defendant may file affidavit of defenses and get action removed.

APPEAL: If more than $50 involved, one can appeal within 10 days to Court of Record for new trial. Must post bond with surety.

WASHINGTON

TYPE: Small Claims.

CLAIM LIMIT: $100 or $200 depending on the classification of the county.

MINIMUM AGE: 18.

STATUTE OF LIMITATIONS: 2–4 years.

FILING FEES: $1 filing fee. $1 plus mileage of 10¢ per mile for personal service.

NORMAL WAITING TIME: Less than one month.

SERVICE OF PROCESS: Personal or registered mail.

VENUE: Where cause of action arose or defendant resides.

ARBITRATION SYSTEM: No provision.

LAWYERS: None allowed unless judge of Justice Court transferred a case where an attorney had filed an appearance to the Small Claims Department.

CORPORATIONS: Corporations may appear as plaintiff or defendant but not through an attorney.

TRANSFER: If counterclaim over jurisdictional limit.

APPEAL: None if claim less than $100 or party wishing to appeal elected to go to Small Claims Court.

COMMENTS: Seattle Court: King County Court House, 3rd Floor, 344-4350; Spokane Court: Public Safety Bldg., 456-2230; Tacoma: Ninth Floor, County City Bldg., 593-4550.

WEST VIRGINIA

TYPE: Justice of the Peace.

CLAIM LIMIT: Less than $300 plus interest.

MINIMUM AGE: 18.

STATUTE OF LIMITATIONS: 2–4 years.

FILING FEES: $5 filing plus $2.50 service on each defendant.

NORMAL WAITING TIME: 20 days.

SERVICE OF PROCESS: Constable or deputy.

VENUE: Judicial district where defendant resides or cause of action arose.

ARBITRATION SYSTEM: Voluntary arbitration system. May appeal to Circuit Court.

LAWYERS: May appear but not required.

CORPORATIONS: May appear as plaintiff or defendant with or without an attorney.

TRANSFER: No provision.

APPEAL: May appeal within 10 days if more than $15 involved. Must post bond of double the amount of judgment.

COMMENTS: Justice of the Peace Court system.

WISCONSIN

TYPE: Small Claims.

CLAIM LIMIT: Less than $500.

MINIMUM AGE: 21.

STATUTE OF LIMITATIONS: 2–6 years.

FILING FEES: $2 clerk's fee plus $2.50 suit tax; 50¢ for regular mail service or $1.50 for certified mail.

NORMAL WAITING TIME: Around 6 weeks.

SERVICE OF PROCESS: Mail service may be used except in eviction actions. Personal service by sheriff or constable may be used.

VENUE: Where cause of action arose or defendant resides.

ARBITRATION SYSTEM: There is a provision for an informal hearing with a clerk.

LAWYERS: May appear but not required.

CORPORATIONS: May appear as plaintiff or defendant with or without an attorney.

TRANSFER: No provision.

APPEAL: Appeal must be taken to the Circuit Court within 20 days of notice of judgment (rent action 10 days). A $5 suit tax and $5 filing fee must be paid. Appeal stays judgment only if a bond is posted for judgment and costs. Circuit Court decisions may be on the record or a new trial may be had in whole or in part.

COMMENTS: Either party may demand jury trial on payment of $24 jury fee, $11 surtax, and $6 additional clerk's fees. On demand of jury trial a written complaint must be served. Madison Court: City Hall, 210 Monona Ave., 266-4341; Milwaukee Court: 276-5800 Ext. 467.

WYOMING

TYPE: Justice of the Peace.

CLAIM LIMIT: Less than $100 for informal procedure.

MINIMUM AGE: 21.

STATUTE OF LIMITATIONS: 1–4 years.

FILING FEES: $1.50 plus $0.60 for mail service.

NORMAL WAITING TIME: Varies throughout state.

SERVICE OF PROCESS: Registered mail for less than $100.

VENUE: Where cause of action arose or defendant resides.

ARBITRATION SYSTEM: Provision for voluntary arbitration.

LAWYERS: May appear but not required.

CORPORATIONS: May appear as plaintiff or defendant with or without attorney.

TRANSFER: No provision.

APPEAL: Claims greater than $25 may be appealed to the District Court. Appeal must be taken within 15 days by paying all costs plus $1.50 transcript fee or giving a bond for double the cost. A new trial is given in the District Court. Appellant may request a jury trial in the District Court within 10 days after the transcript is filed by payment of a jury fee of $12. Appeal stays the execution of judgment only if appellant posts a bond set by the Justice of the Peace up to double the amount of the judgment and not less than $50.

TYPICAL FORMS AND DOCUMENTS

Defendant Summons
Affidavit of Service
Writ of Execution
Court Order for Appearance of Judgment Debtor
Order to Show Cause
Plaintiff's Statement to Clerk
Subpoena
Notice to Appeal
Counterclaim of Defendant
Motion to Vacate

Civil Court of The City of New York

111 Centre Street, New York, N. Y. 10013

Small Claims Part, County of New York

Telephone: 566-3824

To ....

....

ask judgment in this Court against you for $................. together with costs upon the following claim:

There will be a hearing upon this claim on..........................., at 6:30 P.M., in the Small Claims Part Courtroom, Ground Floor, 111 Centre Street, County of New York.

You must appear and present your defense and any counterclaim you may desire to assert at the hearing at the time and place above indicated (a corporation must be represented by an attorney). Unless you do, judgment will be entered against you by default. If your defense or counterclaim, if any, is supported by witnesses, account books, receipts, or other documents, you should produce them at the hearing. The clerk, if requested, will issue subpoenas for witnesses without fee therefor.

If you admit the claim, but desire time to pay, you must appear personally on the day set for the hearing, state to the court that you desire time to pay and show your reasons for desiring time to pay.

🖝 Corporation defendants and Voluntary Associations must appear by attorney. See Section 321A—C.P.L.&R.

IN WITNESS WHEREOF, I have hereunto subscribed my name and affixed the seal of the Court this .... day of ....,

....
Chief Clerk

Attorney for Claimant ....

Address and Telephone ....

If you desire a jury trial, you must, at least one day before the day upon which you have been notified to appear, file with the clerk of the court, a demand for a trial by jury. At that time you will have to make an affidavit specifying the issues of fact which you desire to have tried by a jury, and stating that such trial is desired, and demanded in good faith. To obtain a jury trial you will have to pay a jury fee of Twenty Five Dollars, and you will have to file an undertaking in the sum of $50.00 in cash, to secure the payment of any costs that may be awarded against you. Under the law, the Court may award $25.00 additional cost to the plaintiff if a jury trial is demanded, and a verdict is rendered against you.

BRING THIS NOTICE WITH YOU AT ALL TIMES

DECLARATION OF PERSONAL SERVICE	IN THE SMALL CLAIMS COURT OF _____ JUDICIAL DISTRICT COUNTY OF LOS ANGELES, STATE OF CALIFORNIA	Case Number

_____ vs. _____

Plaintiff(s)   Defendant(s)

I, the undersigned, say: I was, at the time of the service of the papers herein referred to, over the age of eighteen years and not a party to the above-entitled action; I served the _____

_____

(exact description of document served)°

In the above-entitled action by delivering to and leaving with the hereinafter named person(s) personally a copy thereof, at the address and on the date set forth opposite each name of said person(s), in the County of Los Angeles _____, State of California, to wit:

Name of Person Served°°	Street Address and City Where Served	Date of Service
_____	_____	_____
_____	_____	_____
_____	_____	_____
_____	_____	_____

Fee for service $_____, Mileage $_____, Total $_____

Executed on _____ at _____, California,
            (date)   (place)

I declare under penalty of perjury that the foregoing is true and correct.

_____
Declarant

°If document served was a SUMMONS OR DECLARATION AND ORDER and directed to one of those persons mentioned in Sec. 338 C.C.P., insert notation of compliance with notice as required under Sec. 410 C.C.P.

°°If service is upon a corporation, partnership, or association, state its name and the name and official title of person to whom copy of within is delivered. See Sections 674 C.C.P., where service is made on fictitiously named defendant(s).

DECLARATION OF PERSONAL SERVICE

SDJCF-90 2—55—C8 7-57   C.C.P. 1011, 2015.5

Name, Address and Telephone No. of Creditor

This space for court clerk only

IN THE SMALL CLAIMS COURT OF

_____ JUDICIAL DISTRICT
COUNTY OF LOS ANGELES, STATE OF CALIFORNIA

Plaintiff(s):

Defendant(s):

(Abbreviated Title)

CASE NUMBER

WRIT OF EXECUTION
(Money Judgment)

To the Sheriff or any Marshal or Constable of the County of..:

You are directed to satisfy the judgment described below, with interest and costs and your costs and disbursements, as provided by law. (See reverse side.)

NOTICE TO THE JUDGMENT DEBTOR(S): You may be entitled to file a claim exempting your property from execution. See reverse side.

Judgment Creditor(s): (☐ Additional name(s) stated on reverse side.)

Judgment Debtor(s): (☐ Additional name(s) stated on reverse side.)

Judgment entered in the register of actions on:

Amount of Total Judgment as Entered:

Principal	$_____
Interest	$_____
Costs	$_____
Total	$_____

ADD:
Accrued interest on total judgment as adjusted to payments & partial satisfactions	$_____
Accrued costs (per filed Memo of Costs After Judgment)	$_____
Total judgment & accruals	$_____
Subtract payments & partial satisfactions	$_____
Net balance due before issuance of writ	$_____
Add fee for issuance of writ	$_____
NET BALANCE DUE on date of writ	$_____

Add interest at $............ per day from date of writ to date of levy. (7% per year on lesser of (1) Total Judgment as entered, or (2) Net Balance Due, less fee for issuance of writ)

☐ Notice of sale under this writ has not been requested.
☐ Notice of sale has been requested by: (See name(s) and address(es) on reverse side.)

_____ _____, Clerk

(SEAL)   Dated ....   By_____, Deputy

┌ Mailing Address of Judgment Debtor ┐   ┌ Mailing Address of Judgment Debtor ┐

└ ┘   └ ┘

Form Approved by the
Judicial Council of California
Effective July 1, 1971
EGW785-GC 22—(16)-Gdb 1-72

(See reverse side)
WRIT OF EXECUTION
(Money Judgment)

15 U.S.C. §1673, CCP 682,682.1,
684-688, 690, 690.5(b), 692a,
1032.6, 1032.7, etc.

214

This space for Court Clerk only

| ORDER FOR APPEARANCE OF JUDGMENT DEBTOR | IN The Small Claims Court OF .... JUDICIAL DISTRICT COUNTY OF LOS ANGELES, STATE OF CALIFORNIA | Case Number |

vs.

Plaintiff(s)   Defendant(s)

COURT ORDER FOR APPEARANCE OF JUDGMENT DEBTOR

To

(address of debtor)

It is ordered that you, the above-named judgment debtor, appear personally on

(month, day and year) , at (time) M., in Division (day of week)

at

(address of court)

before a judge of the above-named court, or a referee appointed by him, then and there to answer concerning your property.

Dated

Judge   Commissioner

Failure to appear may subject the party served to arrest and punishment for contempt of Court.

For the purpose of securing an order requiring

, judgment debtor in the above-entitled action,
to appear and answer concerning his property, applicant represents and states: that he is the

judgment creditor in the above-entitled action;
that judgment was entered in the above-entitled action on
against the above-named debtor; that said judgment has not been satisfied; that said debtor's residence or place of business is either in the County of Los Angeles or within 150 miles of the place of trial; (applicable items checked)

☐ that execution may properly be issued at this time upon said judgment;
☐ that execution has been issued and has not been returned;
☐ that the above-named debtor has not been examined;
☐ that the above-named debtor has been previously examined   times;**
☐ that the above-named debtor was last examined on
☐ that affidavit or declaration in support of application for order under section 715 Code of Civil Procedure is filed herewith.

Executed on   , at   , California.

(date)   (place)

I declare under penalty of perjury that the foregoing is true and correct.

Declarant

** "A judgment debtor may not . . . be required to appear and answer more frequently than every four months." (Sec. 714 C.C.P.)
** If required by local court rule.

ORDER FOR APPEARANCE OF JUDGMENT DEBTOR

215

C.C.P. 711 7.L 444

Index No..Year 19..........

Civil Court of The City of New York

COUNTY OF.......................................

Plaintiff	**ORDER TO SHOW CAUSE**
against	
Defendant	

Upon the annexed affidavit of.. sworn to the

.... day of ...., 19........, the plaintiff above named, and on all the proceed-

ings had herein, LET the plaintiff or h ....attorney show cause before me or one of the Judges of this

Court, at Part.............. thereof, to be held at the Courthouse thereof, located at.......................................,

in the County of.., City and State of New York, on the.....................................

day of.................................., 19........, at 9:30 o'clock in the forenoon of that day, or as soon thereafter

as counsel can be heard, WHY an order should not be made, vacating and setting aside the judgment

entered herein, in favor of the plaintiff and against the defendant, on the............day of.............................,

19 ....., and restoring the case to the calendar for trial on a day certain and why such other and further

relief should not be granted as may be just in the premises.

Pending the hearing and determination of this motion and the entry of an order thereon, LET all

proceedings on the part of the plaintiff, h.........attorneys and agents and any Marshal or Sheriff of the

City of New York, for the enforcement of said judgment be stayed.

SUFFICIENT CAUSE THEREFOR APPEARING, LET service of a copy of this order, together with the

affidavit annexed hereto on the plaintiff or his attorneys, on or before the.....................day of.............

.................., 19........, be sufficient.

Dated, ..., 19........

....

*Judge of the Civil Court of
the City of New York.*

1. Please read carefully the instructions appearing below before filling out this form:

   a. If you are suing one or more individuals, give full name of each.
   b. If you are suing a business owned by an individual, give the name of the owner and the name of the business he owns.
   c. If you are suing a partnership, give the names of the partners and the name of the partnership.
   d. If you are suing a corporation, give its full name.
   e. If your claim arises out of a vehicle accident, the driver of the other vehicle must be named, and the registered owner of the other vehicle should also be named.

2. State your name and residence address, and the name and address of any other person joining with you in this action. If this claim arises from a business transaction, give the name and address of your business.

   a. Name_____
   Address_____ Phone No._____
   (street address)   (city or locality)

   b. Name_____
   Address_____ Phone No._____
   (street address)   (city or locality)

3. State the name and address of each person or business firm you are suing:

   a. Name_____
   Address_____
   (street address)   (city or locality)

   b. Name_____
   Address_____
   (street address)   (city or locality)

   c. Name_____
   Address_____
   (street address)   (city or locality)

4. State the amount you are claiming. $_____

5. Describe briefly the nature of your claim:

   _____
   _____
   _____

6. Have you demanded payment of this claim? _____
   (yes or no)

7. Has payment been refused? _____
   (yes or no)

8. If your claim does not arise out of a vehicle accident, give address below where obligation was entered into or was to be performed or where injury was incurred.

   _____
   (street address)   (city or locality)

9. Fill out this section if your claim arises out of a vehicle accident:

   a. Date on which accident occurred: _____, 19____

   b. Street or intersection and city or locality where accident occurred:

   _____

   c. If you are claiming damages to a vehicle, were you on the date of the accident the registered owner of

   that vehicle? _____
   (yes or no)

10. I have received and read the form entitled "Information to Plaintiff".

   _____
                                    Signature

THE PEOPLE OF THE STATE OF NEW YORK,

To..

GREETING:

We Command You, That, all business and excuses being laid aside, you and each of

you appear and attend before Hon...

one of the Judges of the Civil Court of The City of New York, County of

...., Part..................., at the Court Room

SUBPOENA TO TESTIFY of said Court, ..., in said City of New York,

on the.....................day of..., 19..........

at...................o'clock in the forenoon, to testify and give evidence in a certain

action now pending in said Court, then and thereto to be tried between

_____

Landlord or Plaintiff

and

_____

Tenant or Defendant

and for a failure to attend you will be deemed guilty of a contempt of Court, and liable to pay all loss and damages sustained thereby to the party aggrieved, and forfeit FIFTY DOLLARS in addition thereto.

Witness, Hon..one of the Judges of said Civil

Court of The City of New York, County of..,

the.....................day of............................in the year one thousand nine hundred and...................

STATE OF NEW YORK,
CITY OF NEW YORK, } ss.
COUNTY OF...................

....being duly sworn, deposes and says

that ....he is of the age of 18 years and upwards, and that on the.....................day of..................., 19..........

........he served the within subpoena upon..

the witness named therein, by delivering to and leaving with h........ personally a true copy thereof, and at the same time and place exhibiting to h........ the within original, and paying to h........ the sum of..................,

h........ fees for traveling to and from the place where ....he was required to attend in and by the said subpoena, and for one day's attendance thereat, and that ....he knew the said..

to be the individual mentioned and described in said subpoena as such witness.

_____

Sworn to before me this

.....................day of..................................., 19..........

_____

This space for Court Clerk only

<table>
<tr><td>NOTICE OF APPEAL
AND UNDERTAKING
ON APPEAL</td><td>IN The Small Claims Court OF
.... JUDICIAL DISTRICT
COUNTY OF LOS ANGELES, STATE OF CALIFORNIA</td><td>Case Number</td></tr>
</table>

.... vs. ....
Plaintiff(s)   Defendant(s)

Comes now the defendant(s) and appeals from the judgment of the above-named court in the above-entitled action, to the Superior Court of the State of California, in and for the County of Los Angeles.

Dated...

....
Appellant(s)

UNDERTAKING ON APPEAL

Whereas the above-named court in the above-entitled action did on ....,
enter judgment in favor of the plaintiff(s) and against the defendant(s) in the sum of $..............................

Whereas the defendant(s) is about to appeal to the Superior Court of the State of California, in and for the County of Los Angeles;

Now, therefore, the undersigned do hereby undertake and promise that if said judgment is affirmed, in whole or in part, or the appeal from such judgment dismissed, then and in that event, the appellant(s) will pay the amount directed to be paid by said judgment, or the part of such amount as to which the judgment is affirmed, if affirmed only in part, and all costs which may be awarded against appellant(s) on appeal; and that if the appellant(s) does not make such payment within twenty days, or within such additional period as may be provided by rules of the JUDICIAL COUNCIL, after the entry by the clerk of said Superior Court the modification or affirmation of said judgment, that judgment may then be entered, on motion of respondent(s) in his favor and against the undersigned sureties for such amount, together with interest that may be due thereon, costs which may be awarded against the appellant(s) on appeal and also the sum of fifteen dollars as an attorney fee.

Dated...

....
signature   residence address   business address

....
signature   residence address   business address

.... and ....
the sureties named in the above bond, each for himself and not one for the other, says that he is a
.... holder and resident within said County and within said State, and is worth the sums herein-
(freeholder or householder)
above mentioned, over and above all of his debts and liabilities, exclusive of property exempt from execution.

Executed on ...., at ...., California
(date)   (place)

I declare under penalty of perjury that the foregoing is true and correct.

....
Surety   Surety

$.............................. cash deposited in lieu of undertaking. (Sec. 117LL C.C.P.)

NOTICE OF APPEAL AND UNDERTAKING ON APPEAL

C.C.P. 117L., 2015.5

Name, address and telephone no. of plaintiff

This space for court clerk only

Date of hearing_____

| Counterclaim of Defendant | IN THE SMALL CLAIMS COURT OF _____ JUDICIAL DISTRICT COUNTY OF LOS ANGELES, STATE OF CALIFORNIA | Case Number |

_____ ▽ _____
                    Plaintiff(s)   Defendant(s)

I, the undersigned, defendant in the above-entitled action, say: that the plaintiff is indebted to me in the

sum of $_____ for_____

_____

which amount I pray be allowed to the defendant against the plaintiff herein.

Executed on_____ at Los Angeles_____County, California.
              (date)

I declare under penalty of perjury that the foregoing is true and correct.

_____
                                        Signature of Defendant

Received copy of within claim on_____, 19_____.

_____
                                        Plaintiff

DECLARATION OF SERVICE

I served the within claim by delivering to and leaving with the person or persons personally hereinafter
named, a copy thereof, at the address and on the date set forth opposite each name of said person or

persons, in the County of Los Angeles_____ State of California,
to wit:

Name of Person Served°	Street Address and City Where Served	Date of Service
_____	_____	_____
_____	_____	_____

Fee for service $_____, Mileage $_____, Total $_____

Executed on_____ at Los Angeles_____County, California.
              (date)

I declare under penalty of perjury that the foregoing is true and correct.

_____
                                        Declarant

°If service is upon a corporation, partnership, or association, state its name and the name and official title of person to whom copy is delivered.

CLAIM OF DEFENDANT

78C662-SC 10-(4)- Cdb 8-73   C.C.P. 117a, 2015.5

'Address of Person to be served | Space Below for Use of Court Clerk Only

| DECLARATION AND NOTICE OF MOTION TO VACATE JUDGMENT | IN The Small Claims Court OF .... JUDICIAL DISTRICT COUNTY OF LOS ANGELES, STATE OF CALIFORNIA .... | Case Number |

.... vs. ....
Plaintiff(s)   Defendant(s)

I, the undersigned, say: I am the ....
.... in the above-entitled action; that judgment was entered
on .... against ....;
I was not present at the trial and did not notify the court before trial that I could not be present because
....;

I believe I can prove the following facts to support my case, to-wit:
....
....
....

WHEREFORE, I request that said judgment be vacated and the case be tried on its merits.

Executed on .... at ...., California.
                    (date)   (place)

I declare under penalty of perjury that the foregoing is true and correct.

....
(Signature of Declarant)

NOTICE OF MOTION

To..
....

Please take notice that on .... , ... , at .... M., in
                              (day of week)   (date)

Div. ....
                              (address of court)

.... , will move the court for an order

vacating the judgment heretofore entered in this case and for trial forthwith.

Dated..   ....
                                                            (Signature of Moving Party)

COURT ORDER

The above motion is ....   Trial is set for ....

Dated..   ....
                                                                                            Judge

DECLARATION AND NOTICE OF MOTION TO VACATE JUDGMENT

BESTSELLERS
FROM DELL

fiction

- [ ] **BEULAH LAND** by Lonnie Coleman _____ **$1.95** (1393-03)
- [ ] **I HEARD THE OWL CALL MY NAME**
  by Margaret Craven _____ **$1.25** (4369-07)
- [ ] **LAST MAN AT ARLINGTON**
  by Joseph DiMona _____ **$1.75** (4652-03)
- [ ] **THE TAKING OF PELHAM ONE TWO THREE**
  by John Godey _____ **$1.75** (8495-05)
- [ ] **EVENING IN BYZANTIUM** by Irwin Shaw **$1.75** (3150-02)
- [ ] **THE LIBERATED** by Henry Sutton _____ **$1.75** (4808-06)
- [ ] **THE TANGO BRIEFING** by Adam Hall _____ **$1.50** (8517-09)
- [ ] **A FAIRY TALE OF NEW YORK**
  by J.P. Donleavy _____ **$1.75** (3233-03)
- [ ] **OPEN SEASON** by David Osborn _____ **$1.50** (6175-06)
- [ ] **JOSHUA, SON OF NONE**
  by Nancy Freedman _____ **$1.50** (4344-07)

non-fiction

- [ ] **THE ONION FIELD** by Joseph Wambaugh **$1.75** (7350-01)
- [ ] **BE THE PERSON YOU WERE MEANT TO BE**
  by Dr. Jerry Greenwald _____ **$1.75** (3325-02)
- [ ] **LOVE AND WILL** by Rollo May _____ **$1.75** (5027-16)
- [ ] **THE LEGEND OF BRUCE LEE**
  by Alex Ben Block _____ **$1.25** (4811-01)
- [ ] **THE NATIONAL FOOTBALL LOTTERY**
  by Larry Merchant _____ **$1.75** (6182-07)
- [ ] **GOING DOWN WITH JANIS**
  by Peggy Caserta _____ **$1.50** (3194-00)
- [ ] **MEAT ON THE HOOF** by Gary Shaw _____ **$1.50** (5584-03)
- [ ] **PRIVATE LIVES OF PUBLIC ENEMIES**
  by Hank Messick _____ **$1.50** (8519-07)
- [ ] **LIFE WITHOUT DEATH?**
  by Nils O. Jacobson _____ **$1.75** (4815-07)
- [ ] **THE KENNEDY PROMISE** by Henry Fairlie **$1.50** (4428-06)

Buy them at your local bookstore or use this handy coupon for ordering:

| Dell | **DELL BOOKS**
P.O. BOX 1000, PINEBROOK, N.J. 07058 |

Please send me the books I have checked above. I am enclosing $_____
(please add 25¢ per copy to cover postage and handling). Send check or
money order—no cash or C.O.D.'s.

Mr/Mrs/Miss_____

Address_____

City_____ State/Zip_____

*Biggest dictionary value
ever offered in paperback!*

The Dell paperback edition of

THE AMERICAN HERITAGE
DICTIONARY
OF THE ENGLISH LANGUAGE

- Largest number of entries—55,000
- 832 pages—nearly 300 illustrations
  The only paperback dictionary with photographs

These special features make this new, modern dictionary
clearly superior to any comparable paperback dictionary:

- More entries and more illustrations than any other
  paperback dictionary
- The first paperback dictionary with photographs
- Words defined in modern-day language that is clear
  and precise
- Over one hundred notes on usage with more factual
  information than any comparable paperback
  dictionary
- Unique appendix of Indo-European roots
- Authoritative definitions of new words from science
  and technology
- More than one hundred illustrative quotations from
  Shakespeare to Salinger, Spenser to Sontag
- Hundreds of geographic and biographical entries
- Pictures of all the Presidents of the United States
- Locator maps for all the countries of the world

A DELL BOOK $1.25

If you cannot obtain copies of this title from your local bookseller, just
send the price (plus 25c per copy for handling and postage) to Dell Books,
Post Office Box 1000, Pinebrook, N. J. 07058.

• Do you really know •
who you are?

Do you know how you look to others? Do you know all about yourself—even the things you don't want to admit? Do you realize that you could be wrecking your chances for happiness and fulfillment without ever suspecting it?

BE THE PERSON YOU WERE MEANT TO BE offers a dramatically effective new way of taking a good honest look at yourself—and making the changes you want to become a whole new you.

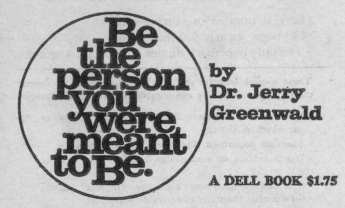

by Dr. Jerry Greenwald

A DELL BOOK $1.75

At your local bookstore or use this handy coupon for ordering:

Dell	DELL BOOKS Be The Person You Were Meant To Be $1.75 P.O. BOX 1000, PINEBROOK, N.J. 07058

Please send me the above title. I am enclosing $_____
(please add 25¢ per copy to cover postage and handling). Send check or money order—no cash or C.O.D.'s.

Mr/Mrs/Miss_____

Address_____

City_____ State/Zip_____

This offer expires 11/75